MATHS PLUS

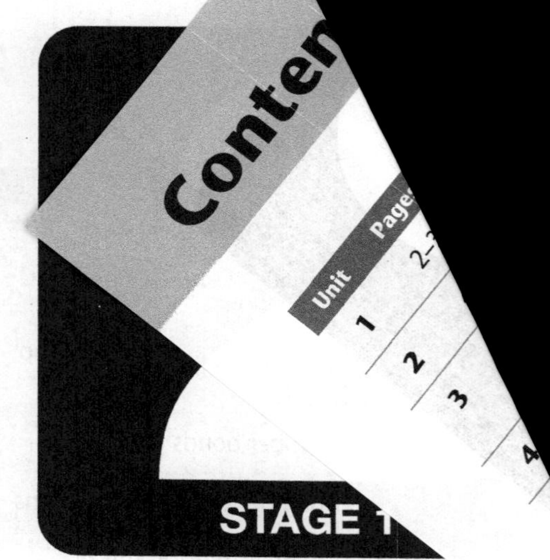

MENTALS AND HOMEWORK BOOK

NEW SOUTH WALES SYLLABUS

Harry O'Brien
Greg Purcell

OXFORD

ts

Contents

NSW Syllabus Outcomes

Units	1	2	3	4	5	6
Number and Algebra						
Representing whole numbers						
MA1-RWN-01 applies an understanding of place value and the role of zero to read, write and order two- and three-digit numbers						
MA1-RWN-02 reasons about representations of whole numbers to 1000, partitioning numbers to use and record quantity values						
Combining and separating quantities						
MA1-CSQ-01 uses number bonds and the relationship between addition and subtraction to solve problems involving partitioning						
Forming groups						
MA1-FG-01 uses the structure of equal groups to solve multiplication problems, and shares or groups to solve division problems						
Measurement and Space						
Geometric measure						
MA1-GM-01 represents and describes the positions of objects in familiar locations						
MA1-GM-02 measures, records, compares and estimates lengths and distances using uniform informal units, as well as metres and centimetres						
MA1-GM-03 creates and recognises halves, quarters and eighths as part measures of a whole length						
Two-dimensional (2D) spatial structure						
MA1-2DS-01 recognises, describes and represents shapes including quadrilaterals and other common polygons						
MA1-2DS-02 measures and compares areas using uniform informal units in rows and columns						
Three-dimensional (3D) spatial structure						
MA1-3DS-01 recognises, describes and represents familiar three-dimensional objects						
MA1-3DS-02 measures, records, compares and estimates internal volumes (capacities) and volumes using uniform informal units						
Non-spatial measure						
MA1-NSM-01 measures, records, compares and estimates the masses of objects using uniform informal units						
MA1-NSM-02 describes, compares and orders durations of events, and reads half- and quarter-hour time						
Statistics and Probability						
Data						
MA1-DATA-01 gathers and organises data, displays data in lists, tables and picture graphs						
MA1-DATA-02 reasons about representations of data to describe and interpret the results						
Chance						
MA1-CHAN-01 recognises and describes the element of chance in everyday events						

Working Mathematically Outcomes

MA1-1WM describes mathematical situations and methods using everyday and some mathematical language, actions, materials, diagrams and symbols

MA1-2WM uses objects, diagrams and technology to explore mathematical problems

MA1-3WM supports conclusions by explaining or demonstrating how answers were obtained

7	8	9	10	11	12	13	14	15	16	17	18	19	20	21	22	23	24	25	26	27	28	29	30	31	32

UNIT 1

Number and Algebra

SET 1 Basic

1 $5 + 1 = \square$

2 $4 + 1 = \square$

3 $3 + 1 = \square$

4 $4 - 1 = \square$

5 $6 + 1 = \square$

6 $8 + 1 = \square$

7 $2 + 1 = \square$

8 $1 + 1 = \square$

9 $7 - 1 = \square$

10 If Tim has 3 cards and Mark has 4, how many do they have altogether? $\square$

SET 2 Ten-frame addition

1 Colour in the ten frames to complete the additions. Complete the answers.

a

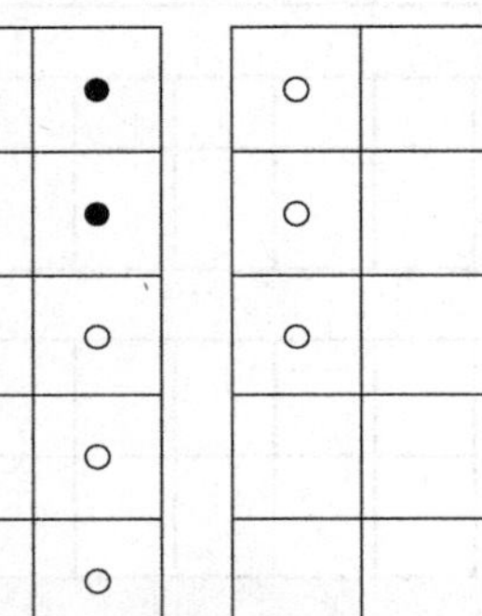

$7 + \square = \square$

b

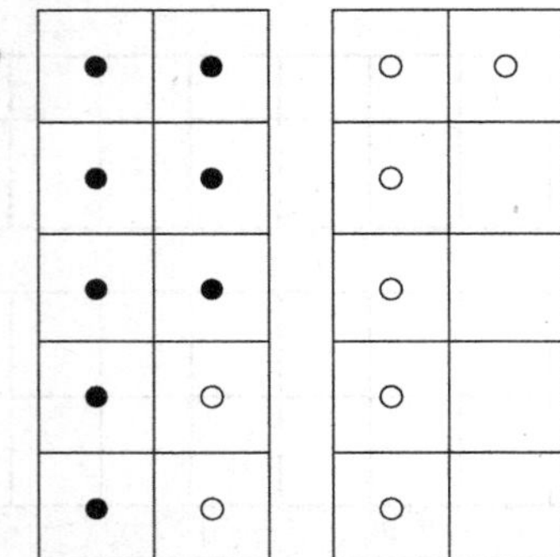

$8 + \square = \square$

2 Complete the Base 10 addition grid.

+	□□	□□□□□	□□□	□□□□□□
□□□□				
□□□□□				
□□□□□□□□				

Space Three-dimensional objects

Join the dots to make 3D objects, then use the words **cube**, **prism** and **pyramid** to name them.

1

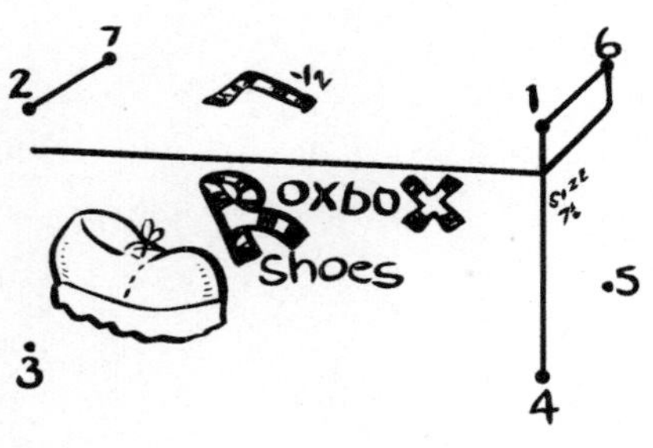

$\square$

2

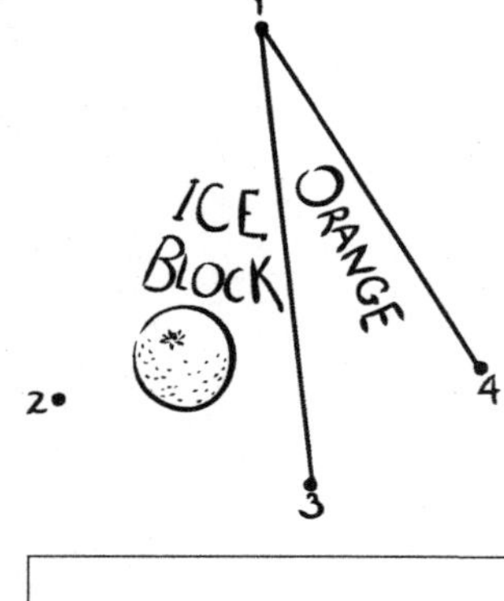

$\square$

3

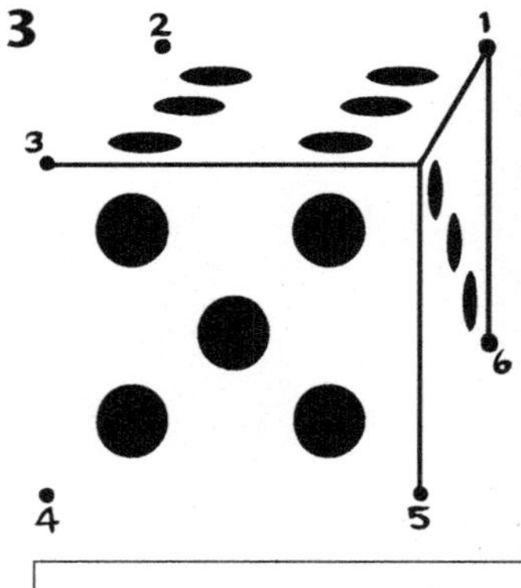

$\square$

Number and Algebra

SET 3 Recreate the whole from the half

Draw the other half to make the whole.

1 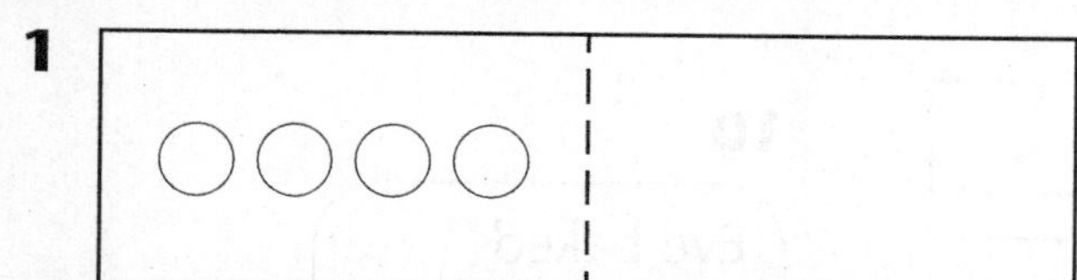

2 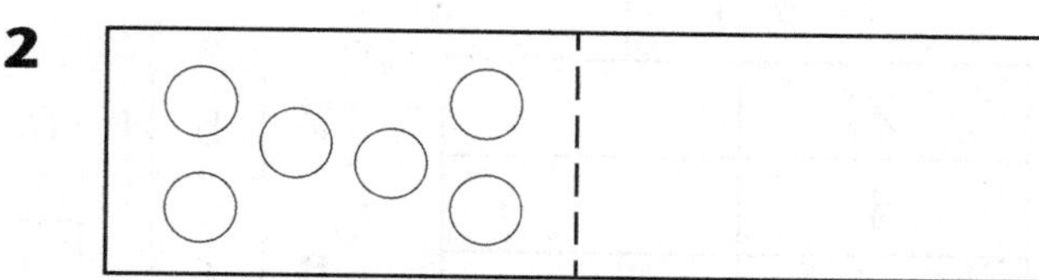

3 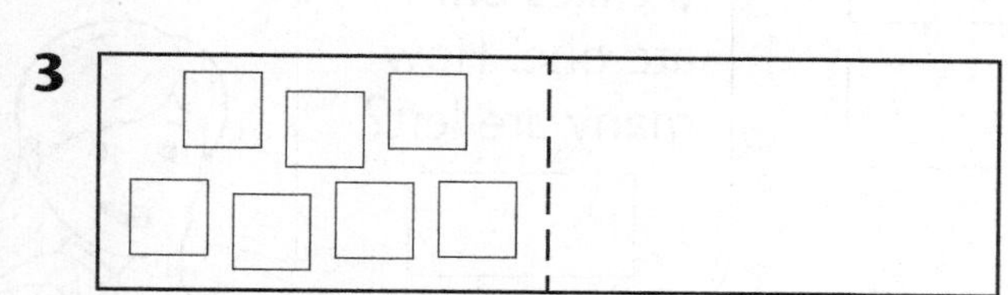

4 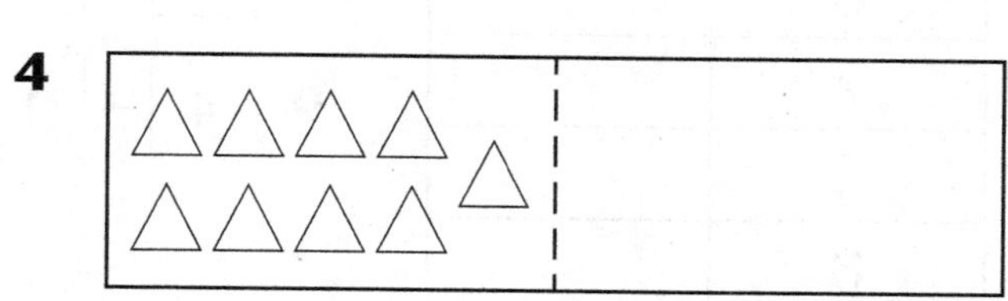

SET 4 Extension

1 [25] = [ ] tens + [ ] ones

2 Which is smaller: 9 + 3 or 4 + 6?

3 How many sides does a square have?

4 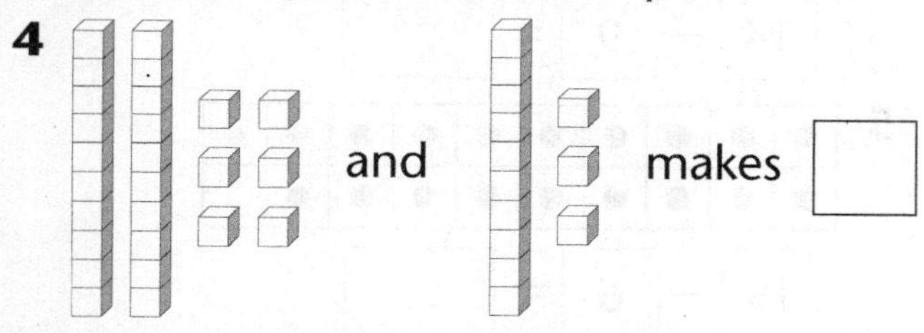
and makes [ ]

5 What is the sum of 9 and 7?

6 [8] tens + [2] ones = [ ]

7 Add $6 to $4.

8 Which number is bigger: 10 + 3 or 9 + 9?

9 Shade two numbers in each circle that total 12.

a 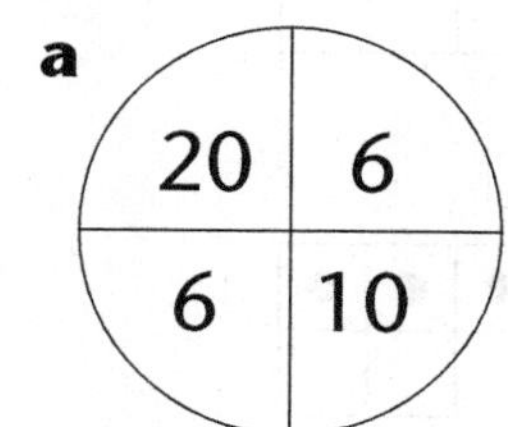

b 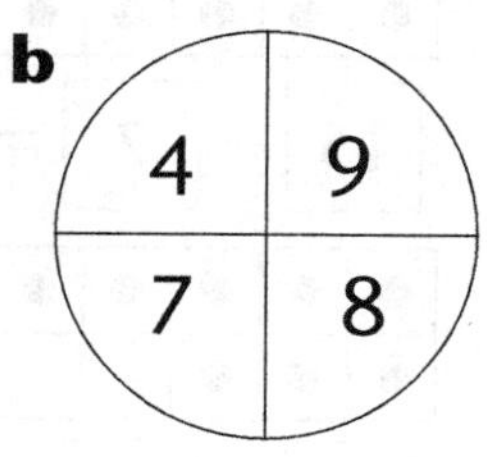

Measurement Informal length units

1 Colour the item that is about the length of 3 paper clips red.

2 Colour the item that is about the length of 4 paper clips yellow.

3 Colour the item that is about the length of 5 paper clips green.

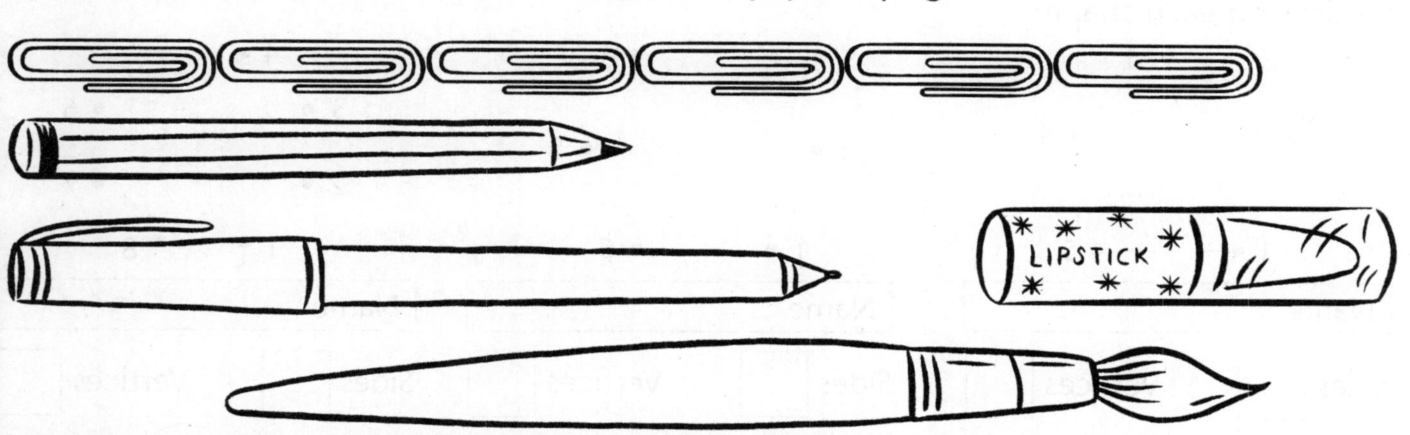

UNIT 2

Number and Algebra

SET 1 Basic

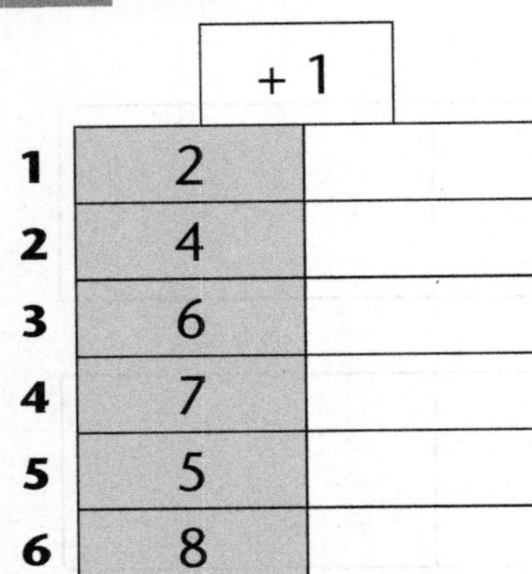

		+ 1
1	2	
2	4	
3	6	
4	7	
5	5	
6	8	

7 8 + 0 = □

8 6 − 1 = □

9 4 − 1 = □

10 Eve baked 6 cakes but ate one. How many are left? □

SET 2 Subtraction strategies

Complete these subtractions.

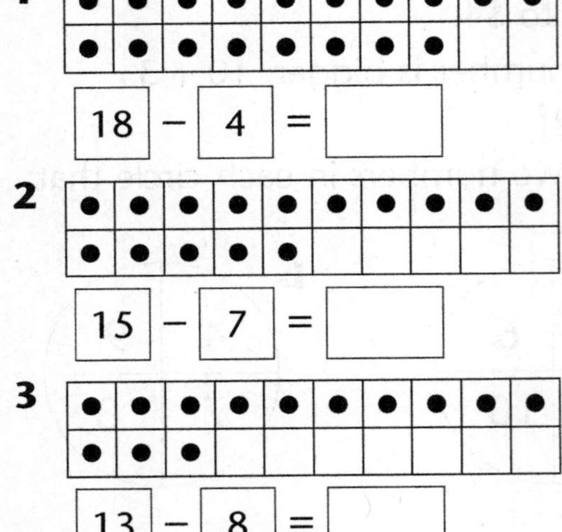

1 18 − 4 = □

2 15 − 7 = □

3 13 − 8 = □

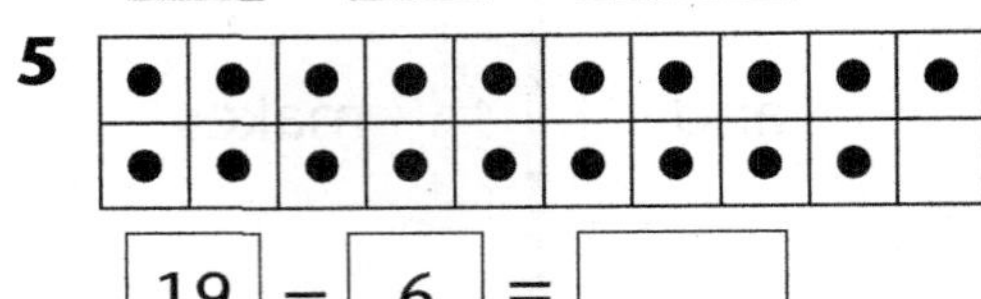

4 14 − 9 = □

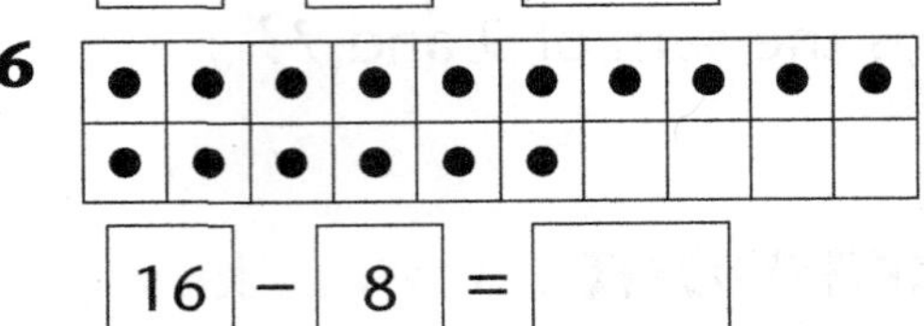

5 19 − 6 = □

6 16 − 8 = □

Space Two-dimensional shapes

Join the dots to form a 2D shape, then name it and record the number of sides and vertices on each shape.

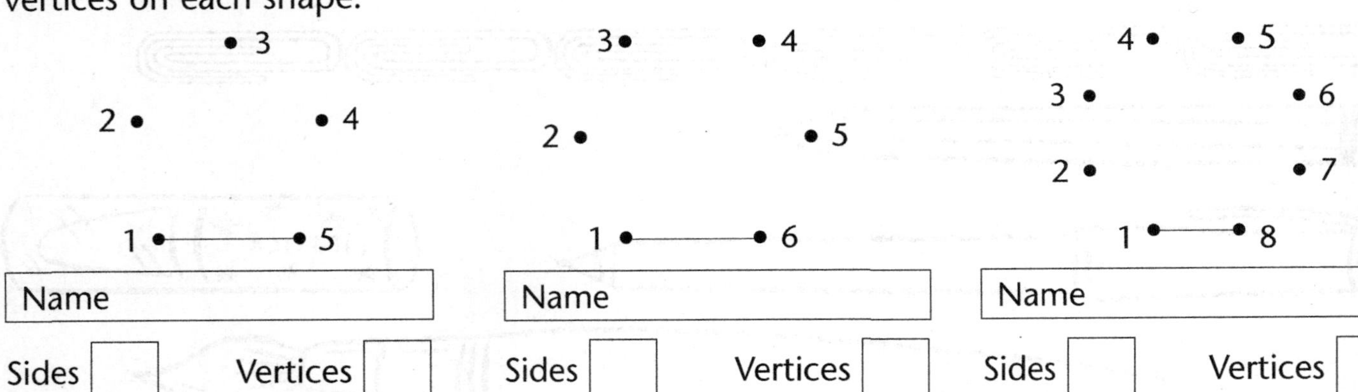

Name □ Sides □ Vertices □

Name □ Sides □ Vertices □

Name □ Sides □ Vertices □

Number and Algebra

SET 3 Skip counting

Continue the skip counting patterns.

1 | 0 | 2 | | | 8 | | 12 |

2 | 0 | 4 | 8 | | | | |

3 | 5 | 10 | | 20 | | | |

4 | 10 | | | | | 60 | |

5 | 10 | 12 | 14 | | | | |

6 | 20 | 25 | 30 | | | | |

7 | 30 | | | 42 | | 50 | |

8 | 50 | | | 65 | | 75 | |

SET 4 Extension

1 8 + 8 = ☐

2 When is Australia Day?

3 Which number is smallest: 267, 672 or 126?

4 8 − 6 = ☐

5 How many 10c coins make 50c?

6 Write the number thirty-six. ☐

7 56 = ☐ tens ☐ ones

8 What is the difference between $17 and $7?

9 What number is between 19 and 21?

10 Complete: 1st, 2nd, 3rd, ____, ____

11 Write three number sentences that have an answer of 5.

a ☐ + ☐

b ☐ + ☐ = 5

c ☐ + ☐

Measurement Area

1 Colour the largest area red and the smallest area green.

2 How could you tell which shape was the largest? ________________

____

a 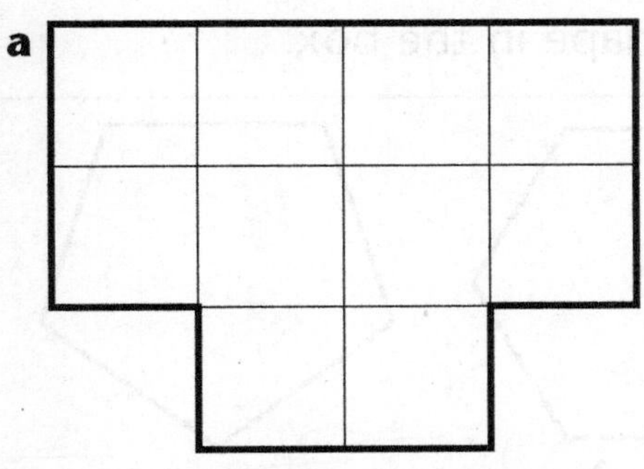

b 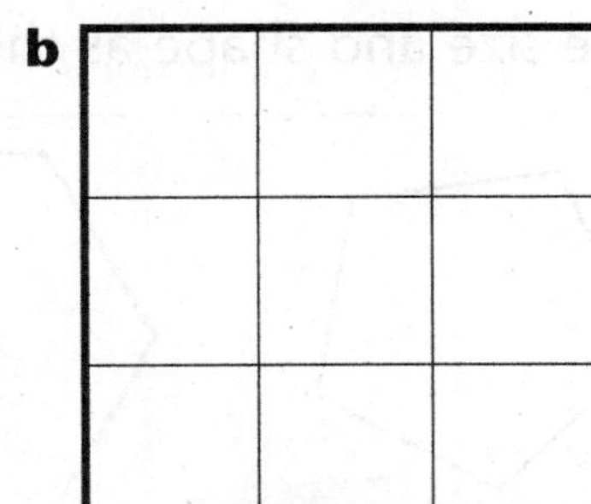

c 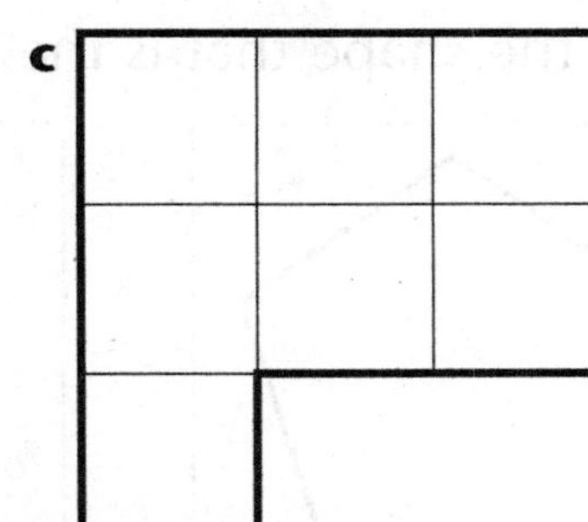

UNIT
3

Number and Algebra

SET 1 Basic

1 2 + 4 = ☐

2 3 + 2 = ☐

3 3 − 2 = ☐

4 4 + 3 = ☐

5 5 − 1 = ☐

6 4 − 2 = ☐

7 2 + 2 = ☐

8 6 − 2 = ☐

9 7 + 1 = ☐

10

Joel and Chris each bought a packet of four lollies. How many do they have between them?

☐

SET 2 Modelling multiplication/skip counting

Skip count to find the totals.

1 ✪ ✪ (5 rows of 2) — 2, ☐, ☐, ☐, ☐

2 ✪ ✪ ✪ ✪ ✪ (5 rows of 5) — 5, ☐, ☐, ☐, ☐

3 ✪ ✪ ✪ ✪ ✪ ✪ ✪ ✪ ✪ ✪ (6 rows of 10) — 10, ☐, ☐, ☐, ☐, ☐

Use skip counting to find out how many shapes there are.

4

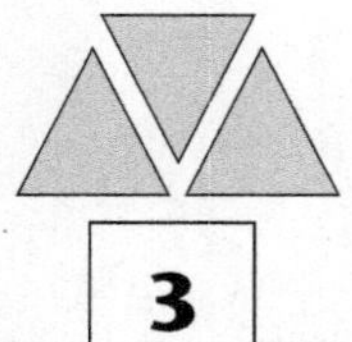

3

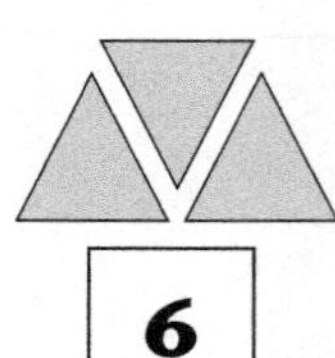

6

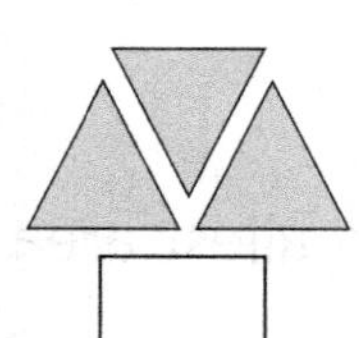

☐

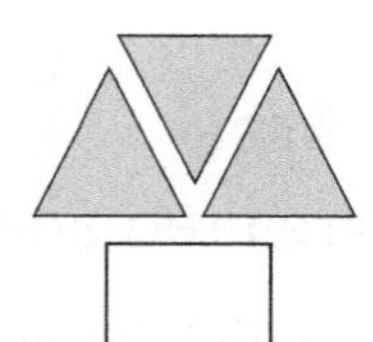

☐

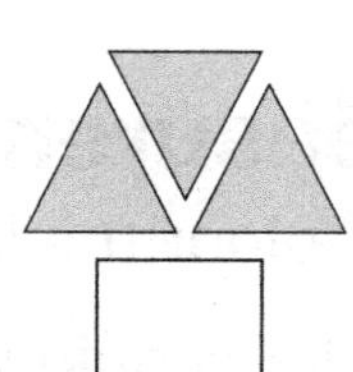

☐

Space Different orientations

Colour the shape that is the same size and shape as the shape in the box.

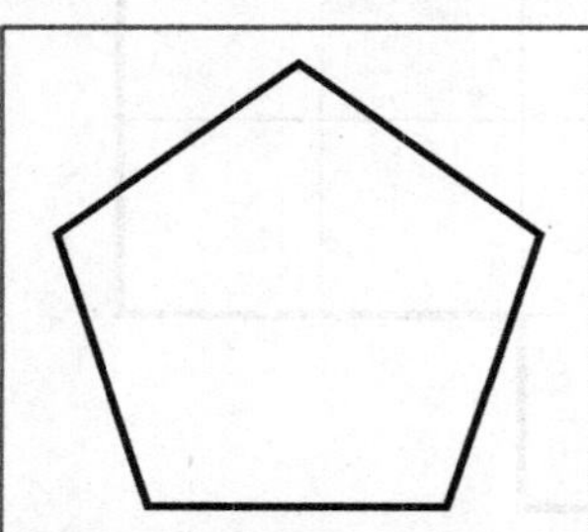

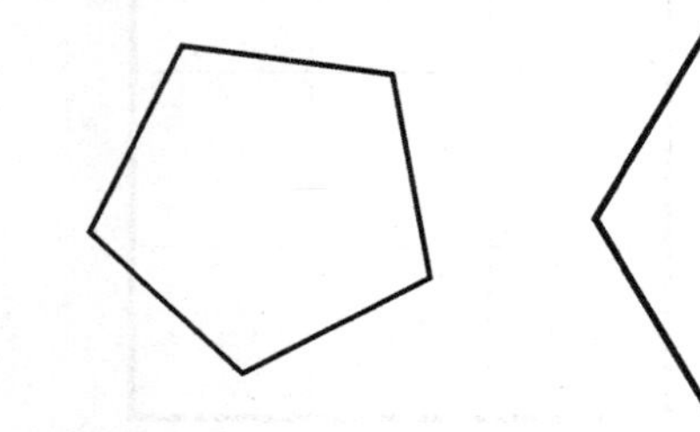

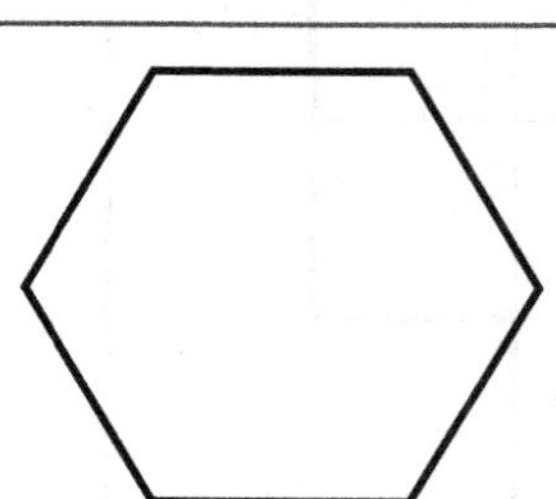

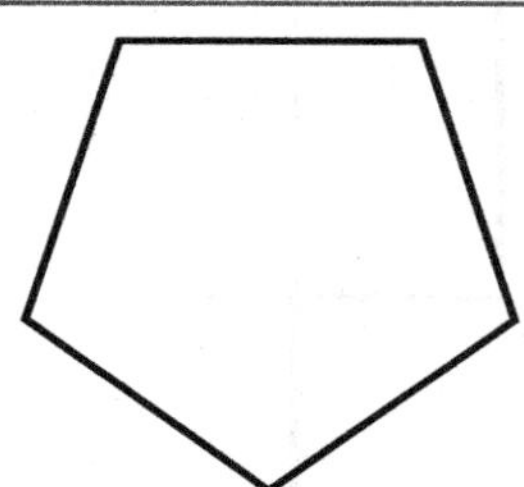

Number and Algebra

SET 3 Numbers to 99

Complete the numeral expanders.

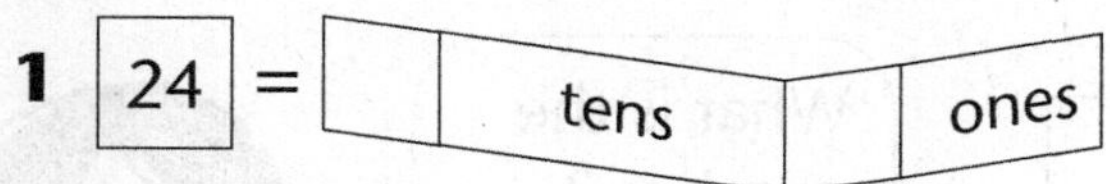

1 24 = ☐ tens ☐ ones

2 32 = ☐ tens ☐ ones

3 56 = ☐ tens ☐ ones

4 12 = ☐ tens ☐ ones

5 28 = ☐ tens ☐ ones

6 99 = ☐ tens ☐ ones

Write the numbers one more and one less than the number in the middle.

7 ☐ 64 ☐ **8** ☐ 96 ☐

SET 4 Extension

1

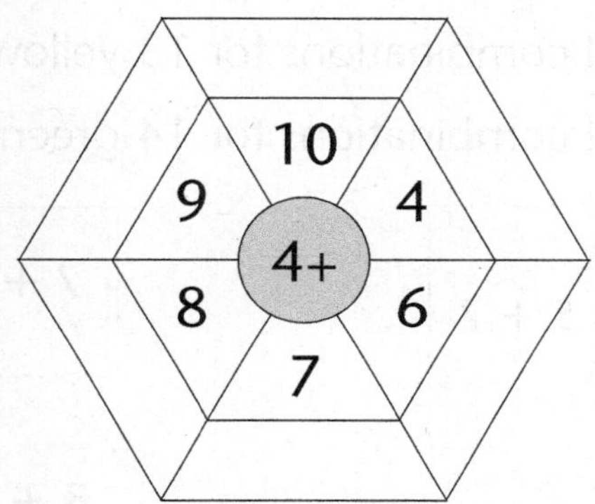

2 Which season comes after autumn?

3 13 + 4 = ☐

4 Subtract 5 from 20.

5 7 + 10 = 17, 17 – 7 = ☐

6 8 × 0

7 What number is between 30 and 32?

8 18 = ☐ tens ☐ ones

9 By how much is 10 less than 17?

10 Circle the smallest number: 215, 512, 125

11 What month is between March and May?

Measurement Half past

Draw the times on the clock faces.

1 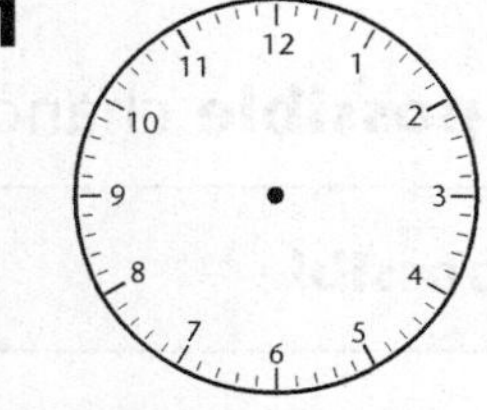

Half past 3

2 Half past 5

3 Half past 9

4 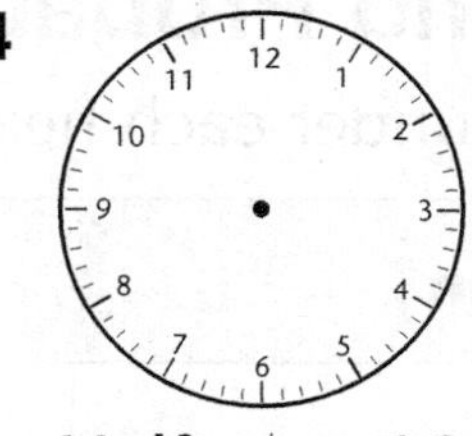

Half past 10

5 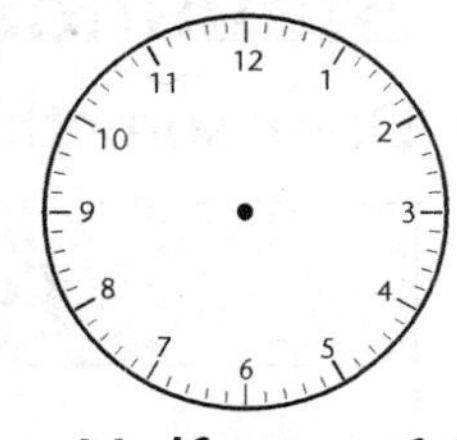

Half past 11

6 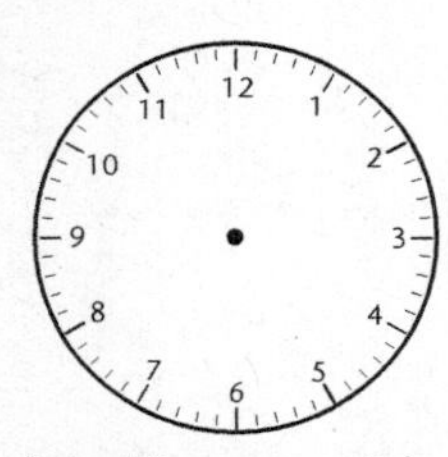

Half past 1

7 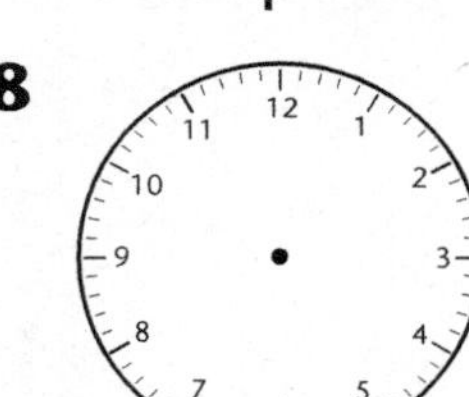

Half past 2

8 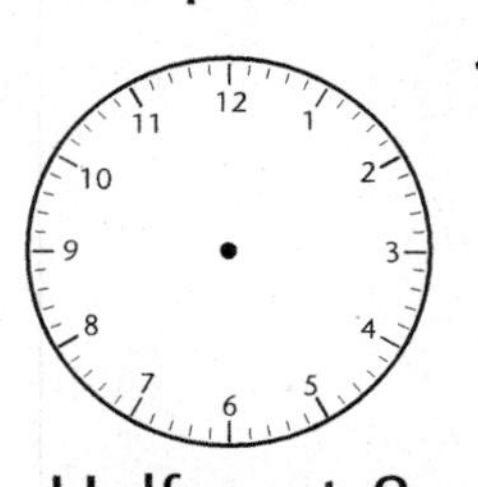

Half past 4

9 Half past 8

10 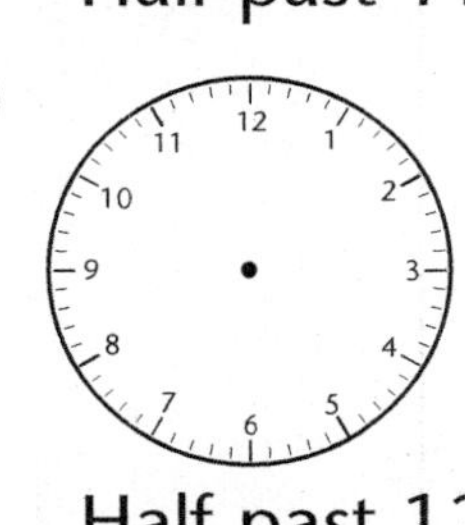

Half past 12

UNIT 4

Number and Algebra

SET 1 Basic

1 5 + 1 = ☐

2 4 + 4 = ☐

3 5 − 2 = ☐

4 5 + 3 = ☐

5 8 − 3 = ☐

6 6 + 2 = ☐

7 4 − 2 = ☐

8 5 − 4 = ☐

9 7 − 2 = ☐

10

What is the number 3 doubled? ☐

SET 2 Number bonds to twenty

1 Colour all combinations for 11 red.

2 Colour all combinations for 12 blue.

3 Colour all combinations for 13 yellow.

4 Colour all combinations for 14 green.

6 + 5

11 + 2

7 + 7

6 + 6

10 + 1

12 + 2

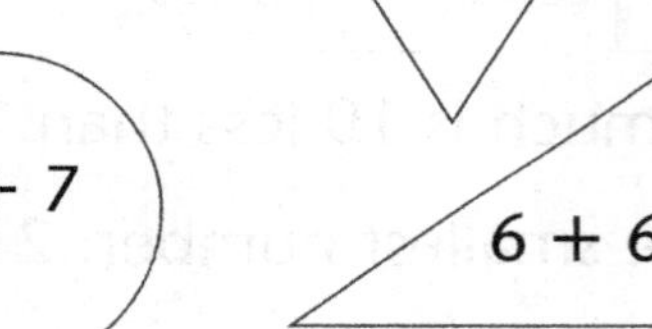

11

12

13

14

5 + 7

10 + 3

10 + 2

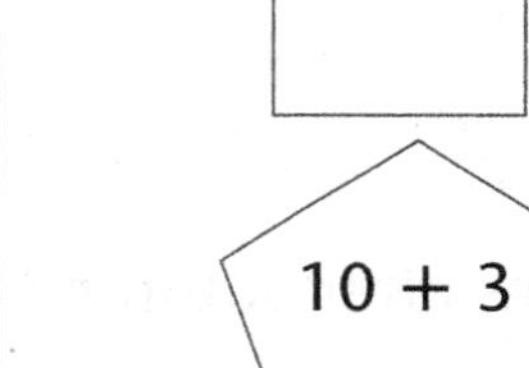

7 + 6

8 + 6

10 + 4

Statistics and Probability Chance events

Draw something under each heading to match **certain**, **possible** or **impossible** chances.

Certain	Possible	Impossible

Number and Algebra

SET 3 Multiplication/groups of

Complete the number sentences.

1 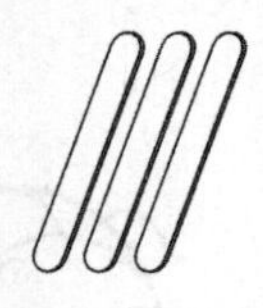 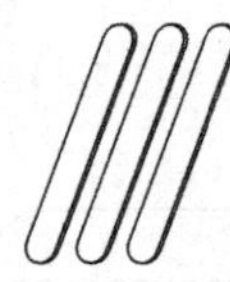 

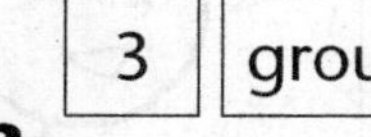

3 groups of 3 = ☐

2  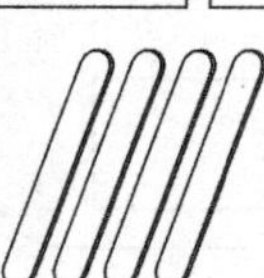 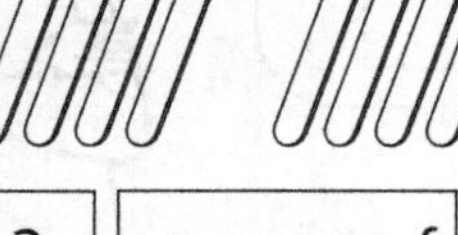

3 groups of 4 = ☐

3  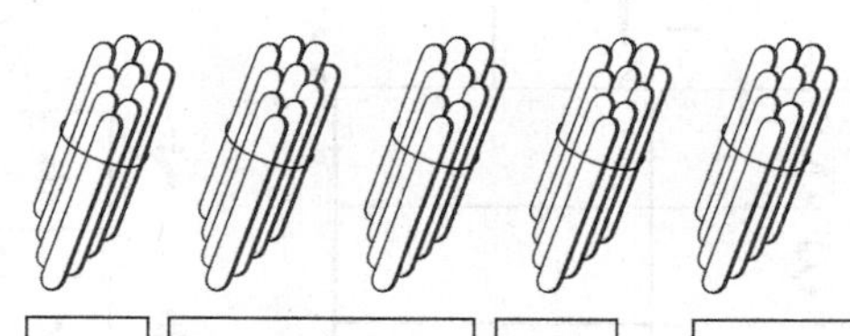

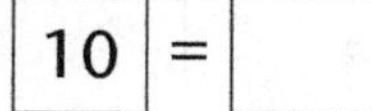

5 groups of 10 = ☐

4 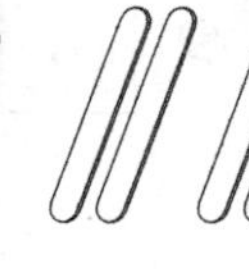

6 groups of 2 = ☐

SET 4 Extension

1 Write the word for 7. ☐

2 How many 10c coins make $1?

3 How many eggs in one dozen?

4 Is 72 odd or even?

5 Which is longer: 1 m or 90 cm?

6 How many days in 2 weeks?

7 A dozen – 5

8 Half of 16

9 6 × 5

10 What month comes before November?

11 How much money is here?

Measurement Ordering capacity

Jan's class measured the capacity of 5 containers using a small plastic cup. They tallied their information.

Juice	卌 II
Bottle	IIII
Jug	卌 卌 III
Mug	II
Vase	卌 I

1 Colour red the vessel that holds the most.

2 Colour blue the vessel that holds the least.

UNIT 5

Number and Algebra

SET 1 Basic

		−1
1	2	
2	3	
3	4	
4	5	
5	6	
6	7	

7 $4 + 1 = \square$

8 $8 - 1 = \square$

9 $6 + 1 = \square$

10

SET 2 Addition to solve subtractions

Count on to find the difference.

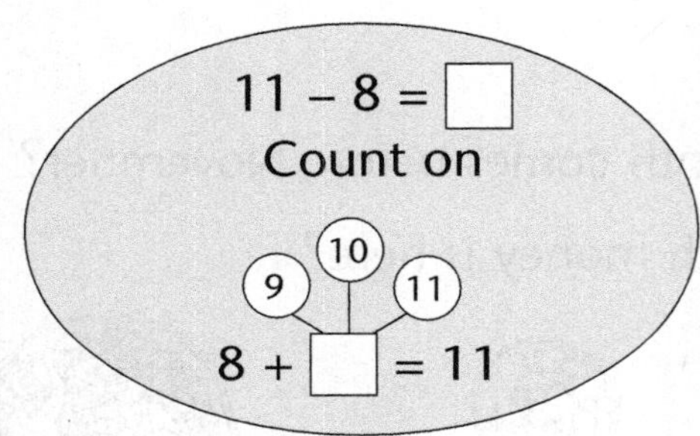

1 $8 - 5 = \square$

2 $7 - 4 = \square$

3 $9 - 3 = \square$

4 $10 - 6 = \square$

5 $19 - 8 = \square$

6 $18 - 6 = \square$

7 $20 - 14 = \square$

8 $15 - 6 = \square$

9

Eve Max

What is the difference in age between Max who is 16 and Eve who is 7 years old?

$\square - \square = \square$

Space Sketching position

Pretend you are looking at the house, then add the objects below.

1 Draw a tree to the **right** of the house.

2 Draw a car to the **left** of the house.

3 Draw a bird **on top of** the house.

4 Put a flower **in front of** the house.

5 Draw an electricity pole **behind** the house. (You won't see all of the pole.)

Number and Algebra

SET 3 Numbers to 1000

Show how many of each of the Base 10 material are needed to make each number.

	Number	Hundreds	Tens	Ones
1	533			
2	652			
3	465			
4	751			
5	963			

5 4 7

6 Use the numbers above to make the largest number you can.

______

7 Use the same numbers to make the smallest number you can.

______

SET 4 Extension

1 What number is three more than 28?

2 10 + ____ = 20

3

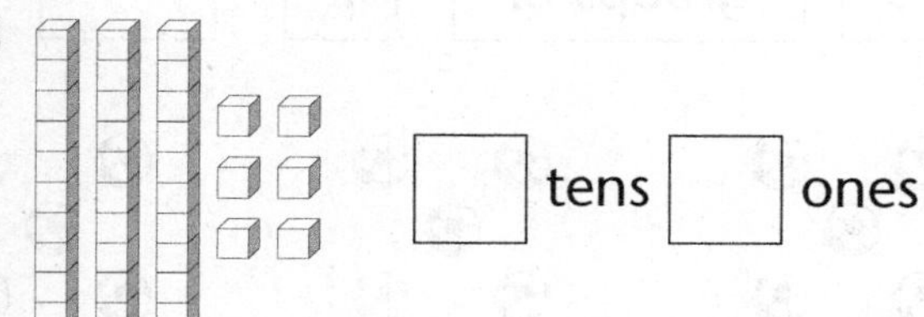

☐ tens ☐ ones

4 What month comes after November?

5 7 + 6 =

6 Max had 13 books but dropped 3. How many does he still have?

7 10 + 11

8 Draw a rectangle.

9 8 – ☐ = 6

10 356 = 3 hundreds ☐ tens ☐ ones

11 Colour in the 2D square.

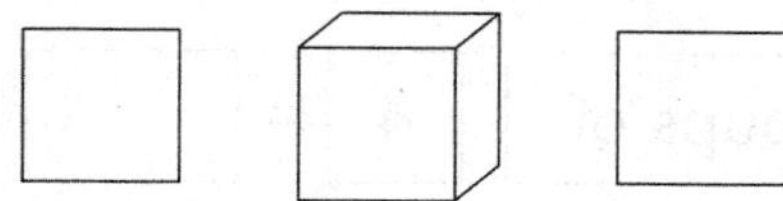

12 How many months in a year?

Measurement Comparing mass

1 What could you use to balance the orange on the scales below?

______

2 Describe how you would measure the mass of the orange.

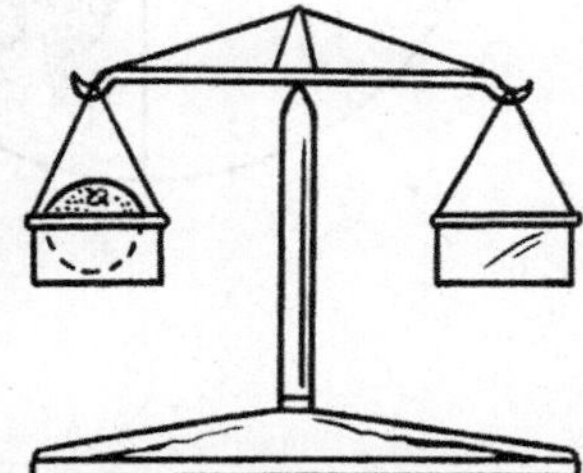

______

______

______

______

______

UNIT 6

Number and Algebra

SET 1 Basic

1 5 + 5 = ☐

2 6 + 3 = ☐

3 8 + 1 = ☐

4 7 − 2 = ☐

5 10 + 2 = ☐

6 8 − 3 = ☐

7 6 + 1 = ☐

8 7 − 2 = ☐

9 5 − 3 = ☐

10 Jayne had four dolls but she lost two at school. How many does she have left? ☐

SET 2 Multiplication/groups of

1 4 groups of 3 = ☐

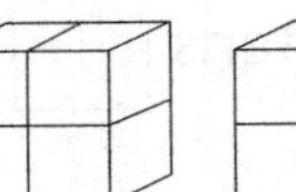

2 4 groups of 4 = ☐

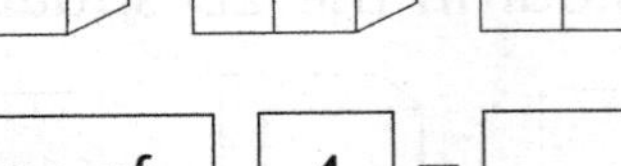

3 5 groups of 2 = ☐

4 3 groups of 5 = ☐

Statistics and Probability Likely/unlikely

1 If the spinner was spun, what would be the most likely colour to come up? ______________

2 Does red have a better chance than blue? ______________

3 Which is the most unlikely colour to come up? ______________

4 Does blue have a better chance than green? ______________

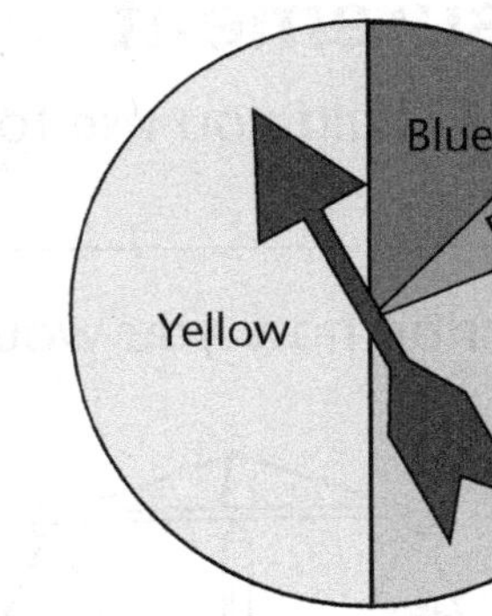

Number and Algebra

SET 3 Repeated addition 1

1

4	groups of	5

☐ + ☐ + ☐ + ☐ = ☐

2

2	groups of	7	= ☐

☐ + ☐ = ☐

3

5	groups of	3

☐ + ☐ + ☐ + ☐ + ☐ = ☐

4

3	groups of	3	= ☐

☐ + ☐ + ☐ = ☐

SET 4 Extension

1 Write a number sentence for the number 16.

☐ + ☐ = 16

2 20, 22, 24, ____, ____

3 Nine take away 3

4 What season comes after summer?

5 | 3 + 7 = 10 | ☐ + ☐ = 10 |

6 13 – 4

7 6 + ☐ = 9

8 20c – 5c =

9 Which is heavier:
1 kg of feathers or 1 kg of stone?

10 20c – 15c =

11 ☐ – 2 = 18

12 What date is Anzac Day?

13 How many sides on one dice?

Statistics and Probability Creating a data table

1 Make a tally of each pet (卌).

cat		bird	
dog		lizard	
fish			

2 Colour the blocks to make a column graph of your tally.

Favourite pets

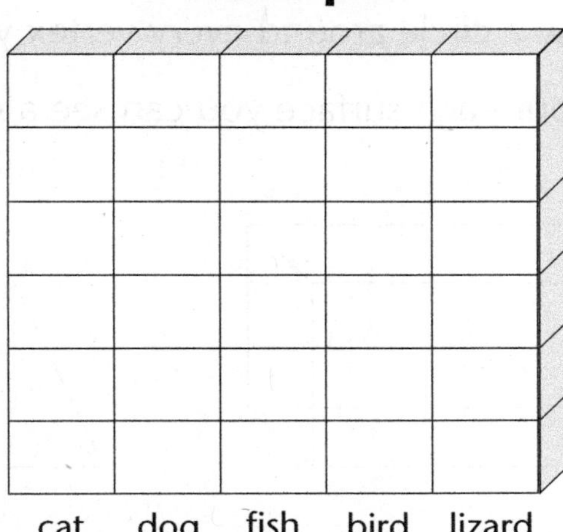

Number and Algebra

SET 1 Basic

	+2	
1	2	
2	3	
3	4	
4	5	
5	6	
6	7	

7. 7 − 2 = ☐
8. 8 + 2 = ☐
9. 10 − 2 = ☐

10

SET 2 Bridging to ten

1. 8 + 3 = ☐
2. 3 + 6 = ☐
3. 9 + 2 = ☐
4. 8 + 4 = ☐
5. 8 + 8 = ☐
6. 9 + 6 = ☐
7. 7 + 4 = ☐
8. 8 + 6 = ☐
9. 6 + 8 = ☐
10. 5 + 7 = ☐

Space Faces, vertices and edges

1. Draw a circle around every vertex you can see.
2. Colour each surface you can see a different colour.

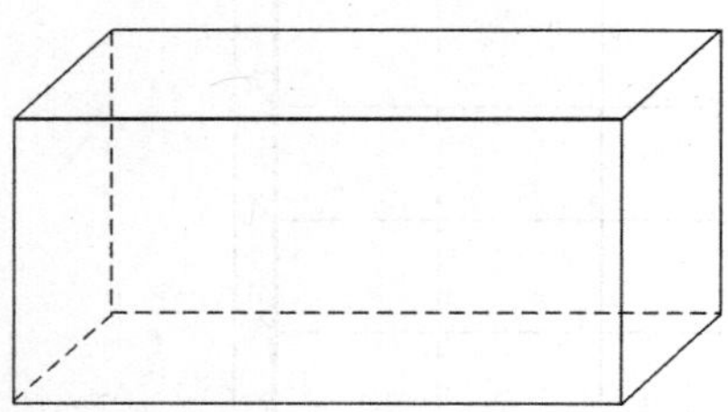
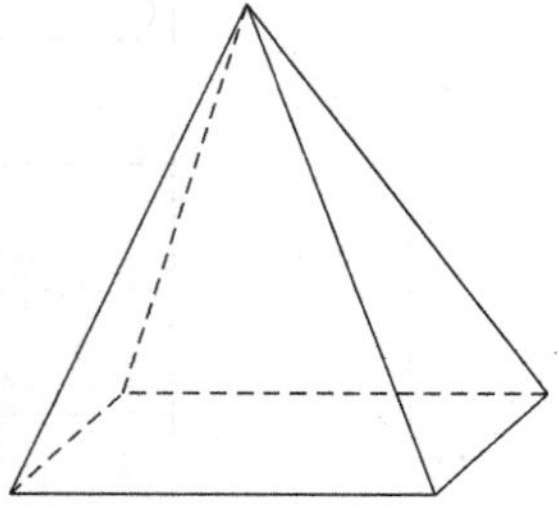
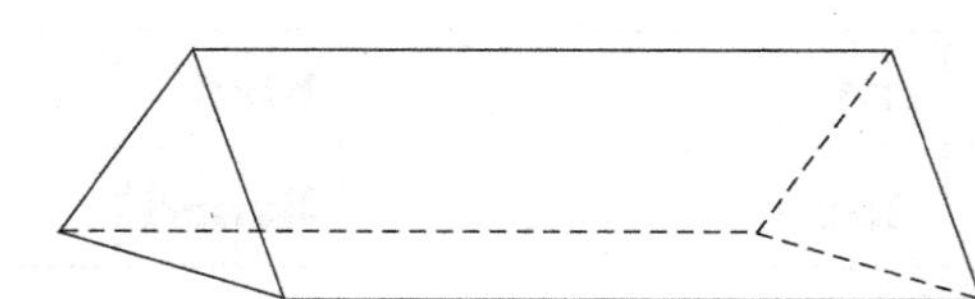

Number and Algebra

SET 3 Place value and ordering

Expand each number on the number expander.

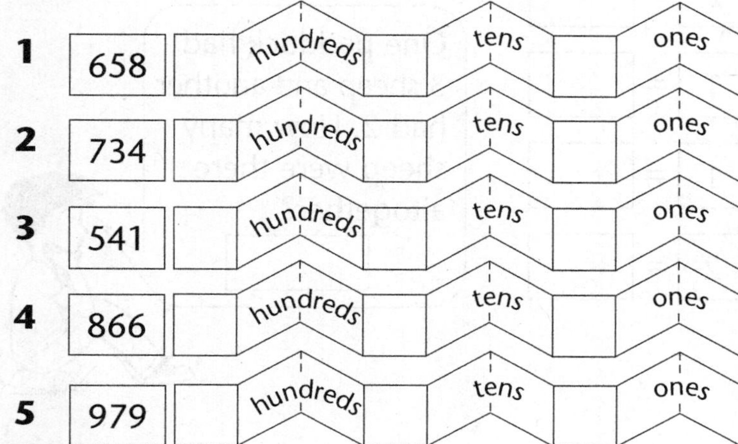

Write the number on each abacus.

6
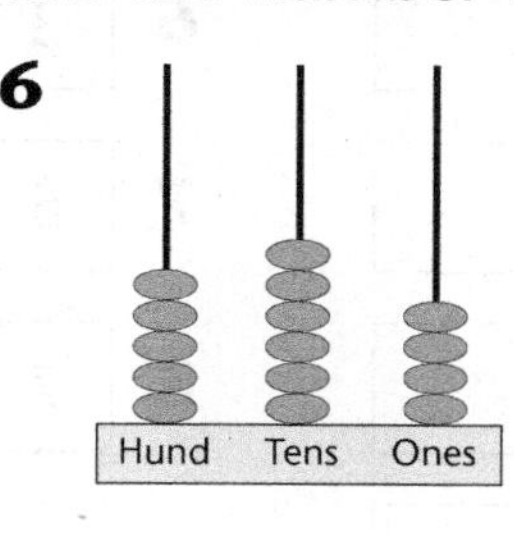

7
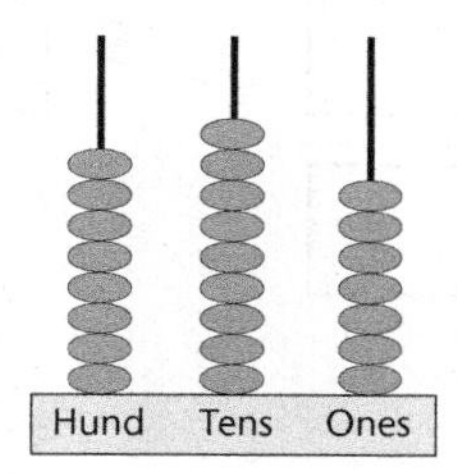

SET 4 Extension

1 Put these numbers in order from smallest to largest: 13, 10, 23, 99

2 20 – ☐ = 6

3 Half of 12

4 7 + 7

5 Add $12 to $8.

6 Is 32 an even number?

7 What is $1 + $0.65?

8 ○○○○○○ ○○○○○○ ○○○○○○ 18 ÷ 3 = ☐

9 What is 6 more than 14?

10 2 × 4

11 Write five number sentences that give the answer 20.

Measurement Time

Draw the times on the clock faces.

1
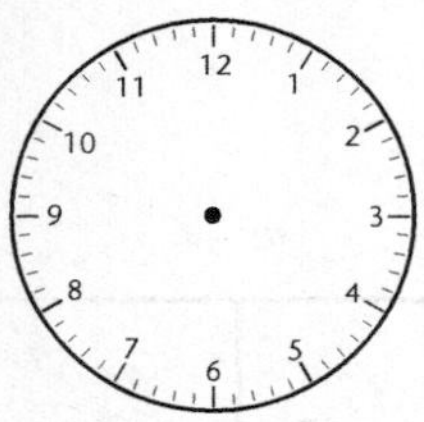

5 o'clock

2
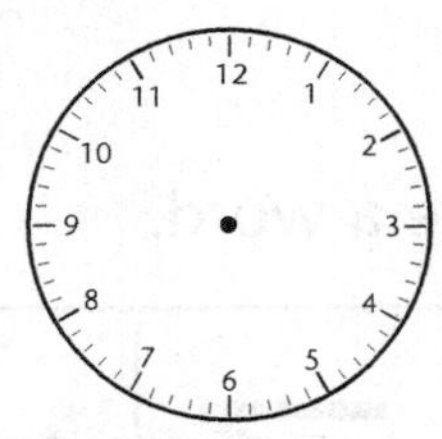

Half past 3

3
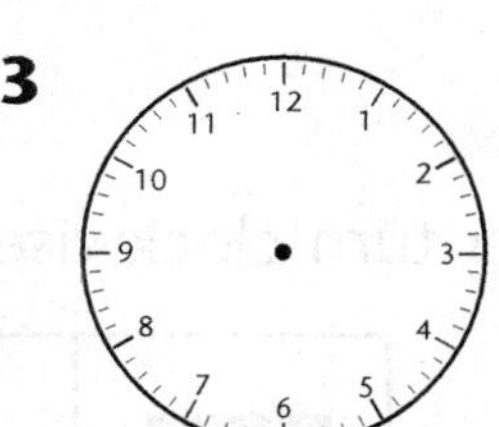

Half past 9

4
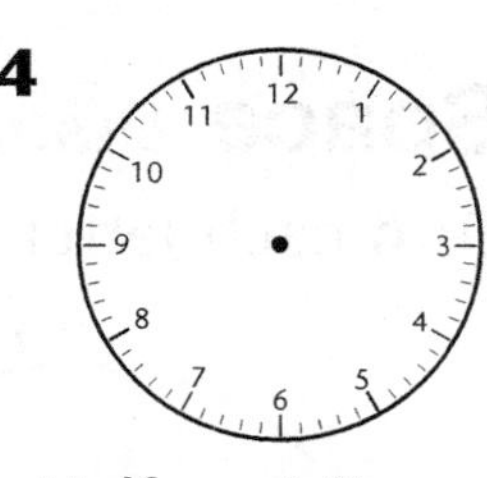

Half past 7

5
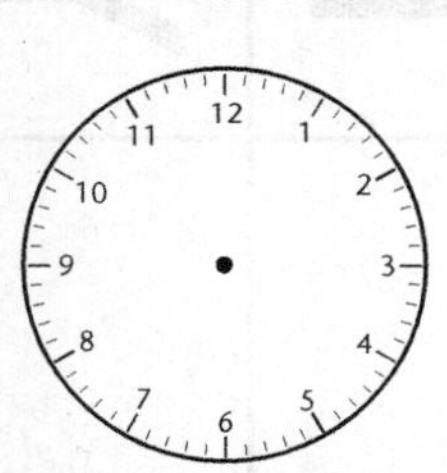

Half past 10

6
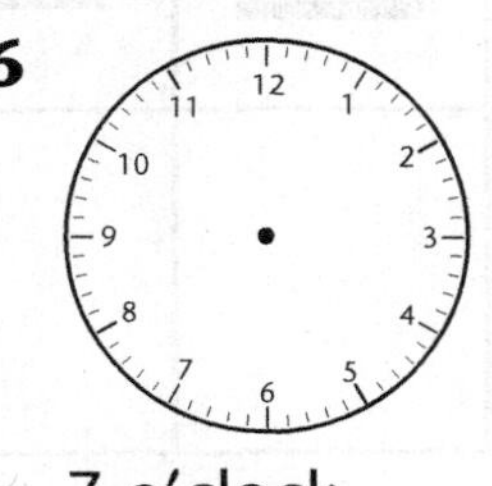

7 o'clock

7
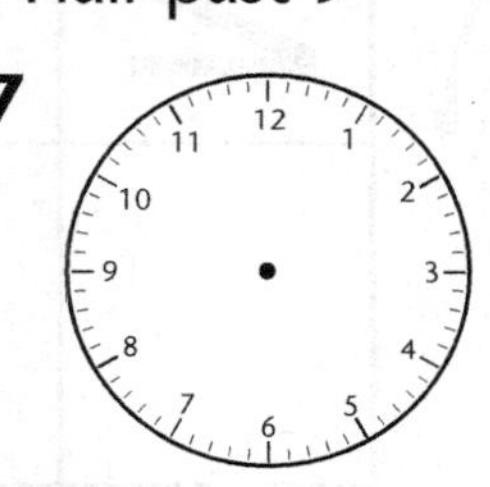

Half past 11

8
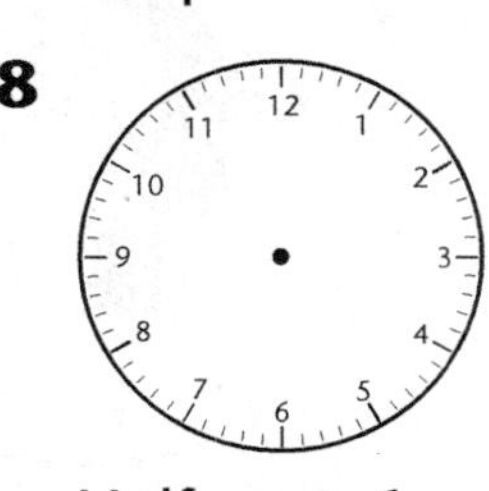

Half past 6

Number and Algebra

SET 1 Basic

1 6 − 1 = ☐

2 2 + 2 = ☐

3 4 − 3 = ☐

4 10 − 6 = ☐

5 4 + 4 = ☐

6 3 + 2 = ☐

7 5 + 1 = ☐

8 7 + 1 = ☐

9 6 + 2 = ☐

10 One paddock had 3 sheep and another had 2. How many sheep were there altogether? ☐

SET 2 Counting on/addition

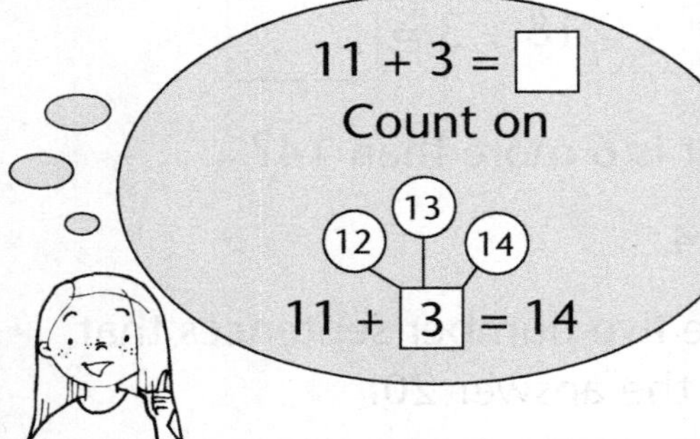

1 6 + 8 = ☐

2 10 + 6 = ☐

3 11 + 8 = ☐

4 12 + 10 = ☐

5 7 + 3 = ☐

6 6 + 6 = ☐

7 10 + 8 = ☐

8 I have climbed 17 stairs but have 8 more to climb. How many stairs are there altogether?

☐ + ☐ = ☐

Space Quarter turns

Turn each letter a quarter turn clockwise to make a word.

Σ	O	N	⋌	Ш	≻

Number and Algebra

SET 3 Doubling and halving

1 What is double 1? ☐

2 What is double 2? ☐

3 What is double 3? ☐

4 What is double 5? ☐

5 What is double 6? ☐

6 What is double 8? ☐

7 What is half 4? ☐

8 What is half 6? ☐

9 What is half 12? ☐

10 What is half 10? ☐

11 What is half 14? ☐

12 What is half 20? ☐

SET 4 Extension

1 Write the words for 310.

2 6 + 2 + 1 = ☐

3 ☐ + 3 + 1 = 8

4 15 – 0 =

5 How many wheels are on 2 cars?

6 Colour in $\frac{1}{4}$ of each shape.

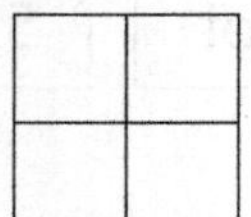

7 How many days are there in May?

8 How many halves are in a whole?

9 Write the number for two hundred and ninety-nine.

10 How many years in a century?

11 What is the fourth month of the year?

12

+	3	6	9	12	15	18	21
3							

Measurement Informal length units

1 How many shoes will fit along the table?

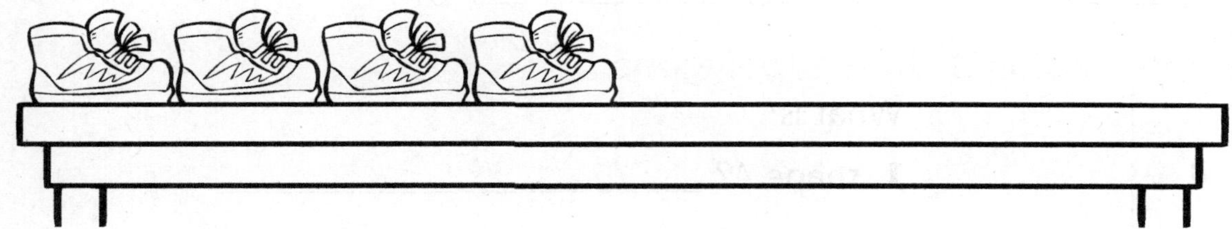

2 How many shoe boxes will fit along the table?

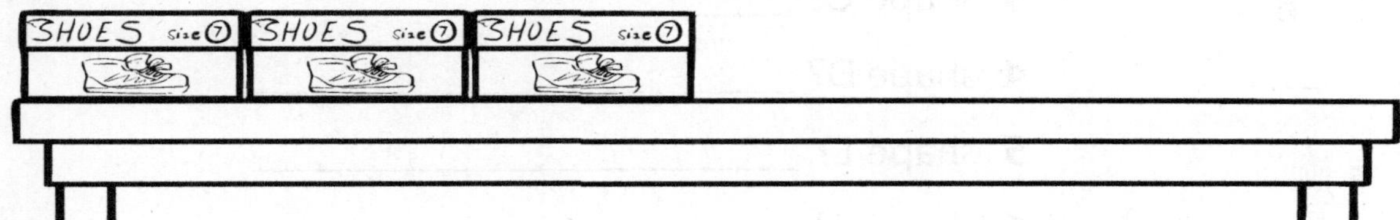

UNIT 9

Number and Algebra

SET 1 Basic

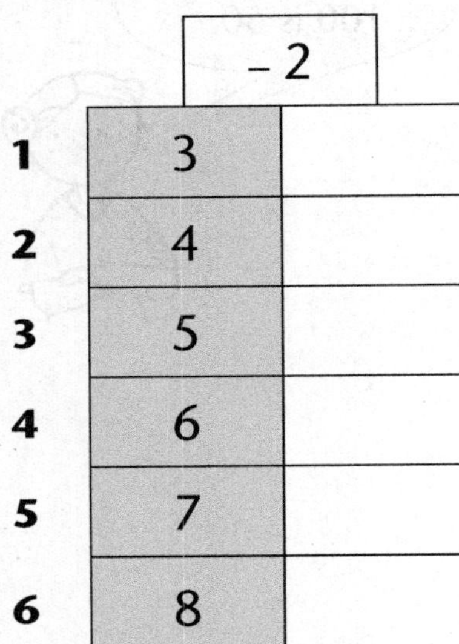

	−2	
1	3	
2	4	
3	5	
4	6	
5	7	
6	8	

7 9 + 2 = ☐

8 7 + 2 = ☐

9 9 − 2 = ☐

10

If Ashley bought two toy cars at one shop and three at another, how many did he buy altogether?

☐

SET 2 Division/equal groups

Circle the groups, then complete the division problems.

1

9 hearts make

☐ groups of 3

2

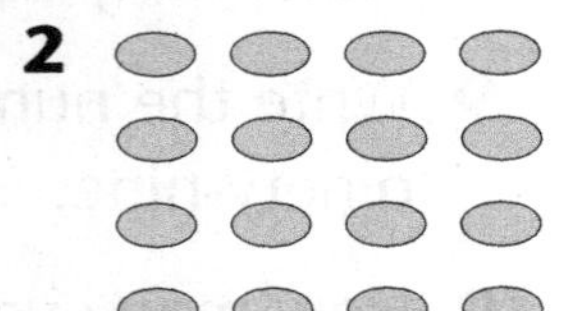

16 ovals make

☐ groups of 4

3

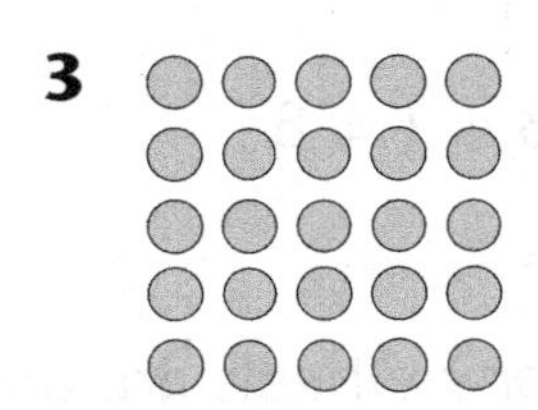

25 circles make

☐ groups of 5

4

15 circles make

☐ groups of 5

5

14 hearts make

☐ groups of 2

Space Two-dimensional shapes/polygons

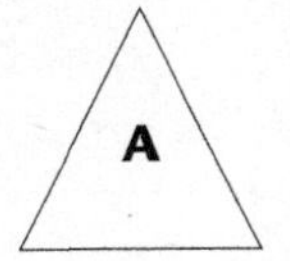

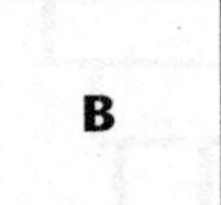

C

D

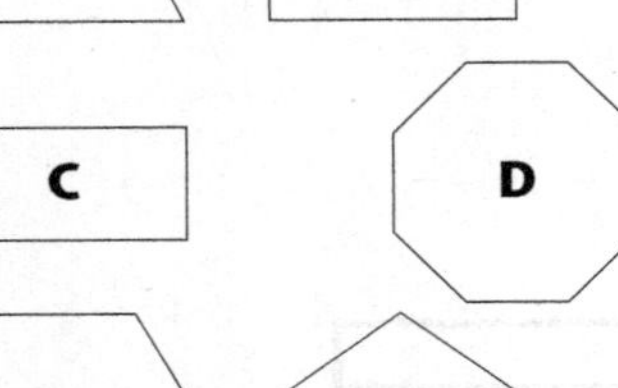

What is:

1 shape A? ____________________

2 shape B? ____________________

3 shape C? ____________________

4 shape D? ____________________

5 shape E? ____________________

6 shape F? ____________________

Number and Algebra

SET 3 Bar models

Use the bar models to help you complete the additions and subtractions.

1 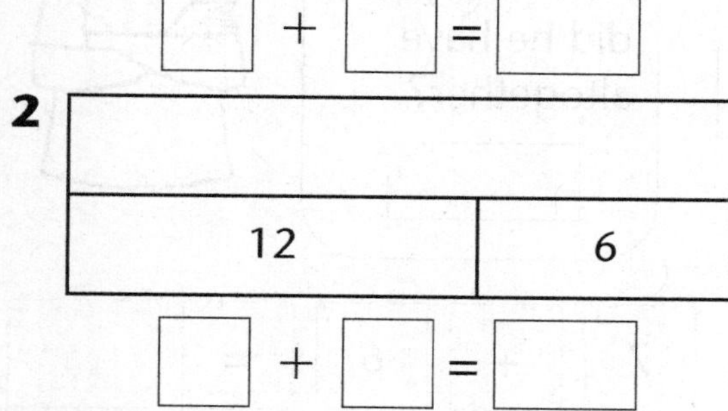

☐ + ☐ = ☐

2

☐ + ☐ = ☐

3 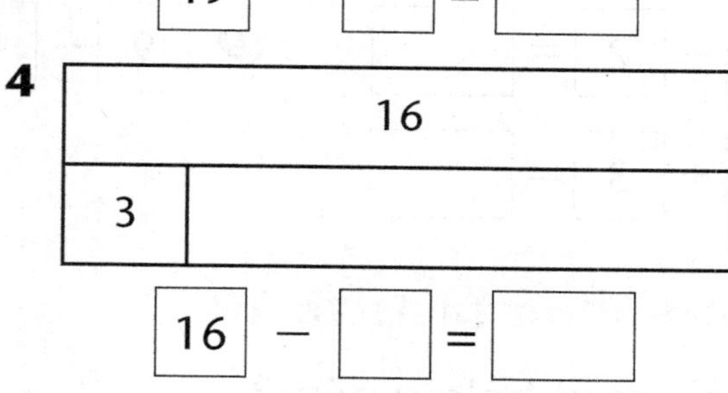

19 − ☐ = ☐

4

16 − ☐ = ☐

SET 4 Extension

1 18 – 9 = ☐

2 10 rows of 4 equals _____.

3 How many legs do 3 birds have?

4 2×3

5 18, 20, 22, _____, _____, _____

6 27 = ☐ tens ☐ ones

7 What number comes after 99?

8 If ♡ = 3, how many does ♡♡♡♡ equal?

9 Draw four rows of 7.

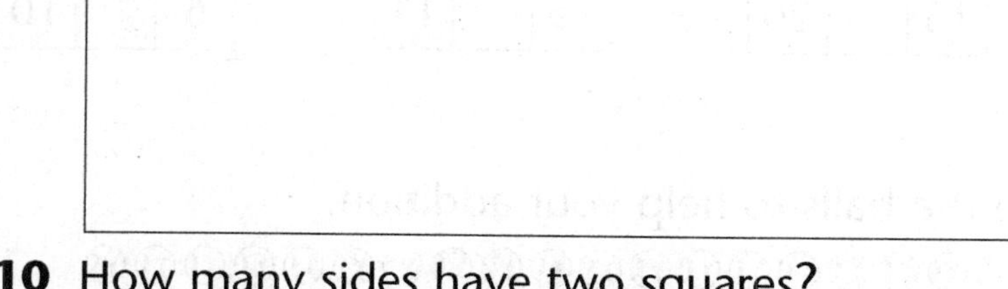

10 How many sides have two squares?

11 What month is Christmas in?

12 21 – 4

13 Two less than 71

Measurement Area

Colour the largest shape red and the smallest blue.

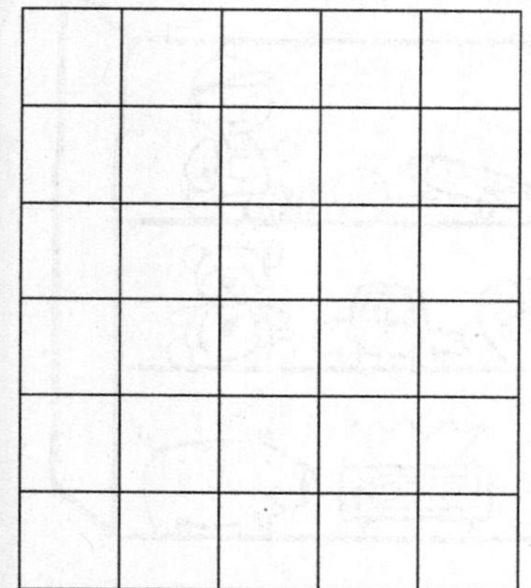

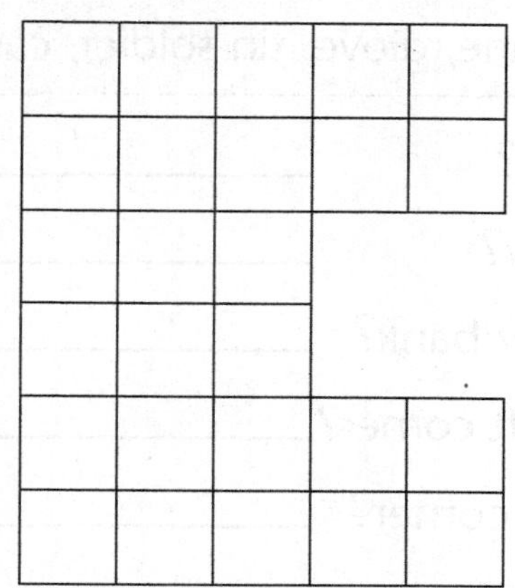

UNIT 10

Number and Algebra

SET 1 Basic

1 3 + 2 = ☐

2 10 + 2 = ☐

3 6 + 1 = ☐

4 7 − 2 = ☐

5 3 + 3 = ☐

6 10 − 2 = ☐

7 4 + 4 = ☐

8 5 − 1 = ☐

9 9 − 4 = ☐

10 Harry had two dogs and four cats as pets. How many pets did he have altogether? ☐

SET 2 Addition facts to 20

1 Which card below wins? ________

a

5		17
	12	
13		20

b

13		18
	17	
15		11

c

19		3
	2	
5		10

2 7 + 6 = ☐

3 10 + 1 = ☐

4 11 + 7 = ☐

5 14 + 3 = ☐

6 9 + 6 = ☐

Use the balls to help your addition.

7 10 + 6 =

8 10 + 10 =

9 8 + 6 =

10 12 + 6 =

Space Position

Use the words to help you answer the questions.

piggy bank, clock, doll, aeroplane, glove, tin soldier, car

1 Which item is above the clock? ________

2 Which item is below the teddy? ________

3 Which item is beside the piggy bank? ________

4 Which item is in the bottom left corner? ________

5 Which item is in the top right corner? ________

Number and Algebra

SET 3 Bridging to ten

Solve the number sentences by bridging to 10.

1	28 +9		+		+		=	
2	49 +8		+		+		=	
3	37 +6		+		+		=	
4	16 +8		+		+		=	
5	35 +8		+		+		=	

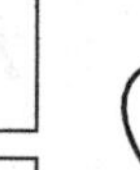

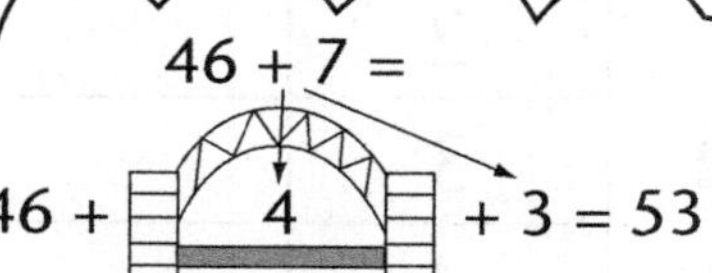

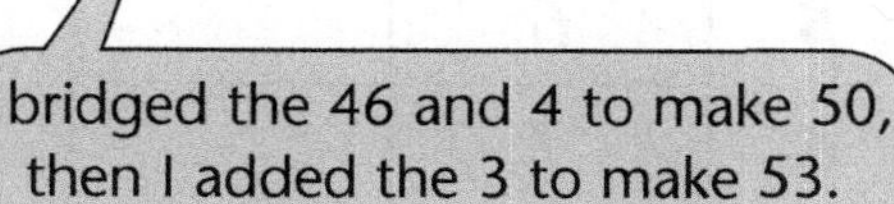

SET 4 Extension

1 3 tens + 6 ones = ☐

2 10 + 11

3 Which is larger: 13 + 2 or 15 – 1?

4 How many months are in a season?

5 22 – 7

6 6 + ☐ = 30

7 30c + 50c =

8 ☐ – 3 = 20

9 2, 4, 6, ____, 10, ____, 14

10 If one bag has 12 apples, how many are in 2 bags?

11 What date is Boxing Day?

12 4 less than 17

13 19 + 2

14 How many days in 2 weeks?

Measurement Duration

Colour the box to show the time it would take to do these things.

1 Wash my hands	**2** Watch a TV show	**3** Eat an apple

☐ 1 minute ☐ 1 hour	☐ 1 hour ☐ 1 day	☐ 5 minutes ☐ 1 hour

Number and Algebra

SET 1 Basic

	+3
1	2	
2	3	
3	4	
4	5	
5	6	
6	7	

7 10 + 5 = ☐

8 15 − 5 = ☐

9 6 + 4 = ☐

10

On Monday, Jenna swam 4 laps in the morning and 10 laps at night. How many laps did she swim altogether? ☐

SET 2 Counting back

Count back to solve these subtractions.

1 15 − 6 = ☐

2 11 − 8 = ☐

3 20 − 9 = ☐

4 14 − 7 = ☐

5 15 − 9 = ☐

6 11 − 3 = ☐

7 20 − 1 = ☐

8 14 − 4 = ☐

Complete the numeral and symbol cards to answer the problems.

9 I had 14 pencils but lost 5.

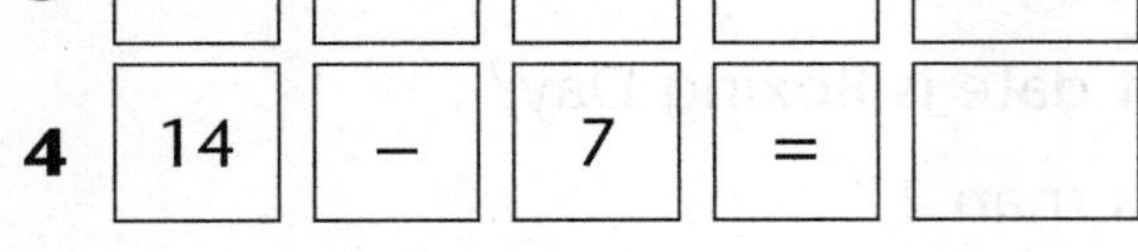

☐ ☐ ☐ = ☐

10 I blew up 13 balloons but 6 burst.

☐ ☐ ☐ = ☐

Space Faces of three-dimensional objects

Colour the correct number of faces for each object.

1

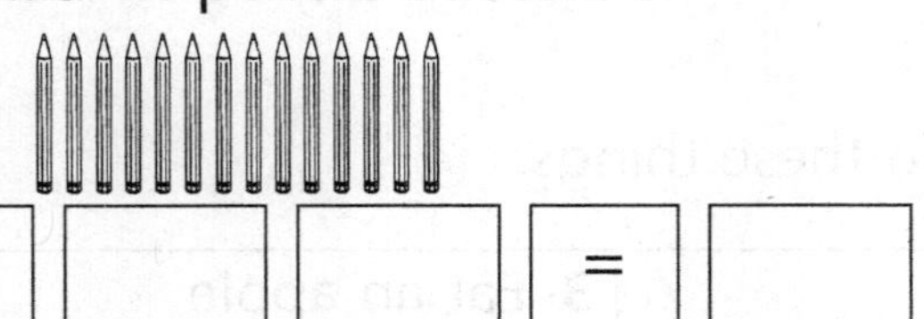

2

Number and Algebra

SET 3 Constant difference

1 Write two number sentences with a difference of 2.

☐ – ☐ = 2   ☐ – ☐ = 2

2 Write two number sentences with a difference of 6.

☐ – ☐ = 6   ☐ – ☐ = 6

3 Write two number sentences with a difference of 5.

☐ – ☐ = 5   ☐ – ☐ = 5

SET 4 Extension

1 52, 62, ____, 82, ____, 102

2 How many quarters in a whole?

3 25 – ☐ = 10

4 What fraction of this shape has been shaded?

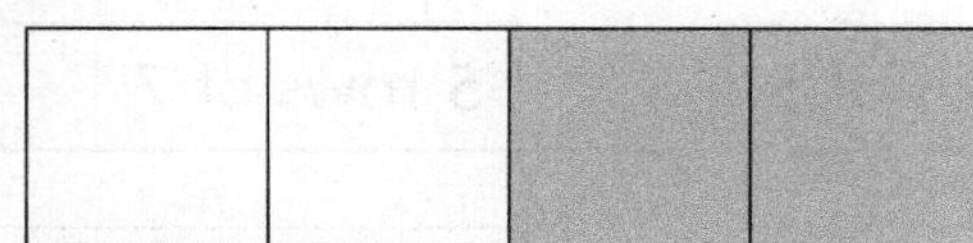

5 How many sides do 4 triangles have?

6 27 + ☐ = 33

7 Jayne had $1.20 but spent $0.70. How much does she have left?

8 Twelve less than 42

9 34, 44, ____, 64, ____, 84

10 36 + 54

11 How many centimetres in 1 m?

12 24 = ☐ dozen

13 Put these numbers in order from smallest to largest. 23, 83, 43, 13, 10, 22

Measurement Volume

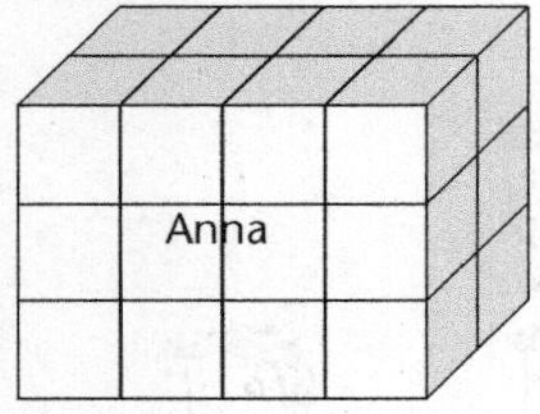

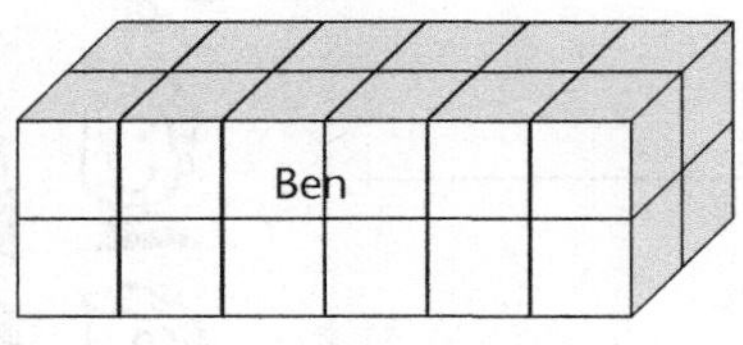

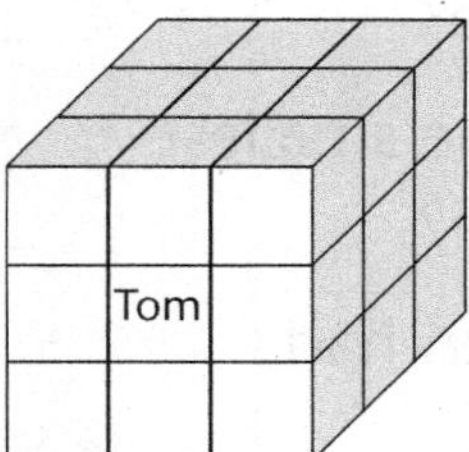

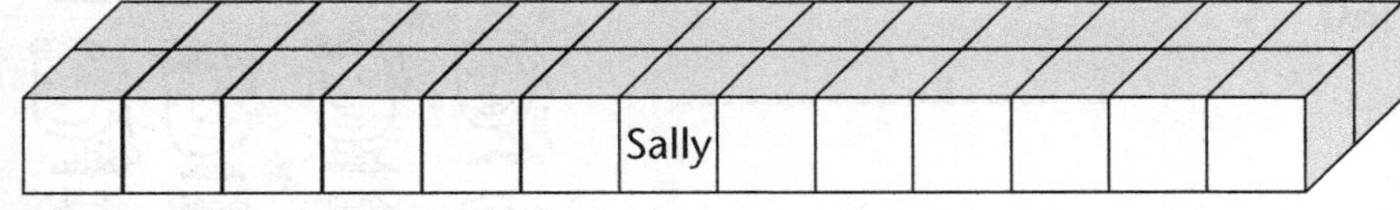

1 Which child made the largest model? ____________________

2 Which child made a model with 26 cubes? ____________________

Number and Algebra

SET 1 Basic

1. 10 + 6 = ☐
2. 10 + 2 = ☐
3. 3 + 3 = ☐
4. 4 + 2 = ☐
5. 10 − 4 = ☐
6. 9 + 1 = ☐
7. 8 − 3 = ☐
8. 10 + 5 = ☐
9. 6 + 6 = ☐
10. If there were 20 cows and 5 were sold, how many were left? ☐

SET 2 Multiplication

Write two multiplication facts for each array.

1 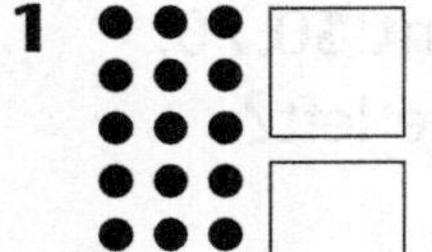 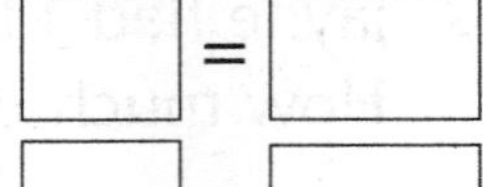 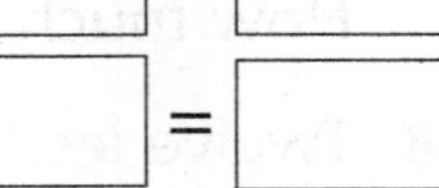

☐ rows of ☐ = ☐

☐ columns of ☐ = ☐

2 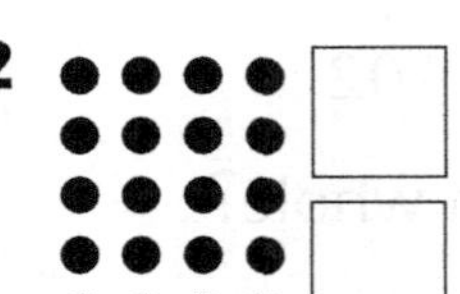 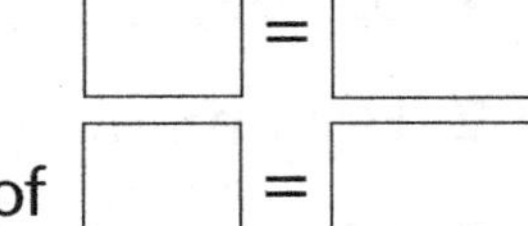

☐ rows of ☐ = ☐

☐ columns of ☐ = ☐

Complete these balanced multiplications.

3	8 rows of 3	3 rows of 8	☐
4	4 rows of 6	6 rows of 4	☐
5	7 rows of 5	5 rows of 7	☐
6	5 rows of 6	6 rows of 5	☐

Statistics and Probability Picture graphs

1. Which hair colour did the largest number of children have? ________
2. Which hair colour did the smallest number of children have? ________
3. How many more children had blond hair than black? ________
4. How many more children had brown hair than fair? ________

Class hair colours

Number and Algebra

SET 3 Division/sharing

Use the arrays to help solve the problems.

1 Share 8 fish into 2 fish ponds.

There are ☐ in each pond.

2 Share 15 frogs into 3 fish ponds.

There are ☐ in each pond.

3 Share 24 dogs into 4 groups.

There are ☐ in each group.

SET 4 Extension

1 What is the coldest season?

2 $\frac{1}{2}$ of 12

3 45 + 12

4 Cents in $1.10?

5 Fifteen less than 45

6 How many 20c coins in $1.20?

7 How many sides does a pentagon have?

8 7 tens 6 ones =

9 14 + 16

10 40, 44, 48, ____, ____

11 How many days in March?

12 99 – 44

13 How many legs on 2 horses?

14 45 + 43

Measurement Comparing capacity

Colour the container you think holds more in each pair.

1

✳

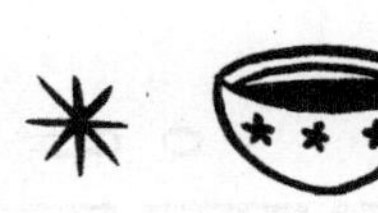

2

✳

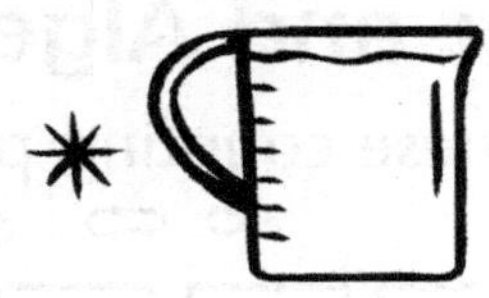

3

✳

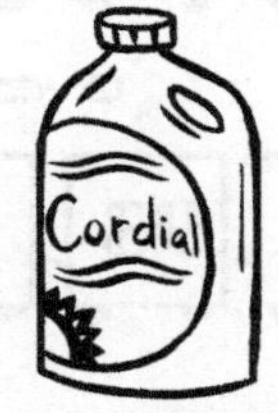

4

✳

Number and Algebra

SET 1 Basic

	+4	
1	2	
2	4	
3	6	
4	10	
5	12	
6	14	

7 7 + 6 = ☐

8 4 − 3 = ☐

9 10 − 6 = ☐

10 Taryn planted 5 trees at school and 10 at the local park. How many did she plant altogether? ☐

SET 2 Addition jump strategies

Use the jump strategy to solve the problems.

1 Courtney had 15 cards and her dad gave her another 15 cards.

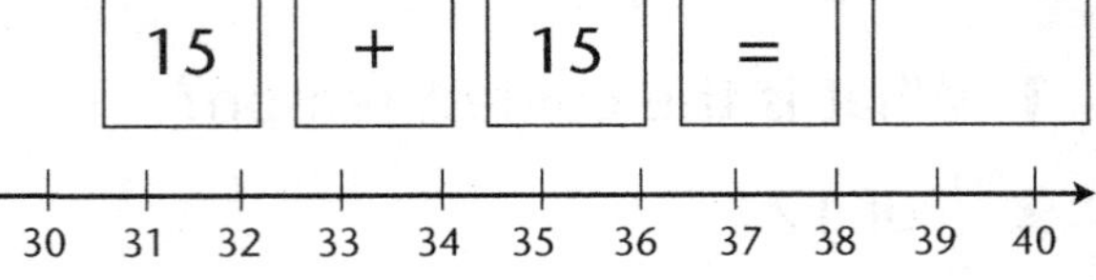

15 16 17 18 19 20 21 22 23 24 25 26 27 28 29 30 31 32 33 34 35 36 37 38 39 40

2 How many children were on the bus if there were 32 girls and 19 boys?

32 + 19 = ☐

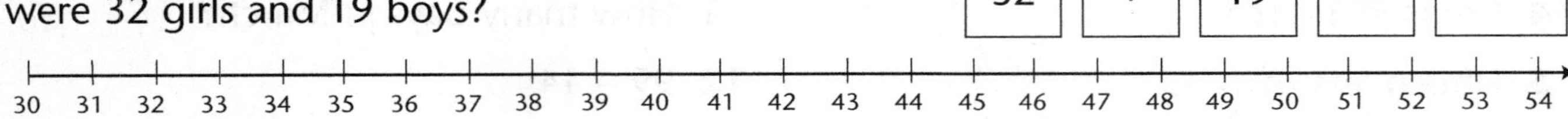

3 Tom scored 28 points in the first game and 24 points in the second. How many points did he score altogether?

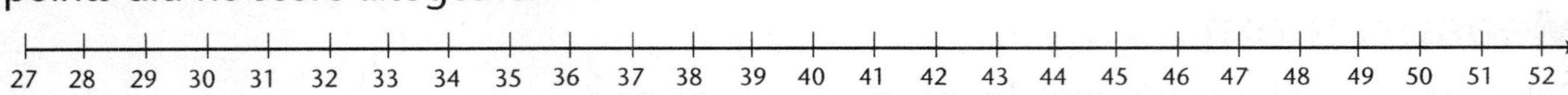

Number and Algebra Counting patterns

Continue these counting patterns.

Number and Algebra

SET 3 Number patterns

Complete the counting patterns.

1	86	88	90			
2	10	14	18			
3	85	90	95			
4	12	14	16			
5	205	210	215			

Fill in the missing numbers in these number patterns.

6	32		36		40	42			48
7		30	35		45		55	60	
8	85		75	70		60		50	
9	86		82		78		74		70

SET 4 Extension

1 27 + 4

2 32 – ☐ = 23

3 8 tens plus 3 ones

4 How many sides on a triangle?

5 How many sides on 7 triangles?

6 How many hours in one day?

7 Which month comes before October?

8 60 – 12

9 Colour $\frac{3}{4}$ of these shapes. 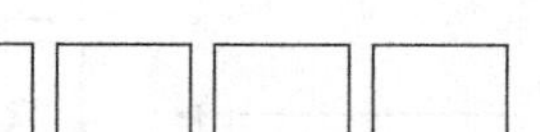

10 If this month is January, what month will it be in 3 months' time?

11 Change from $2 if I spent 50c

12 10 + ☐ = 56

13 54 + 20

14 In what position did the fish come?

1st 2nd ☐ 4th

Measurement Informal mass units

The mass of each item was measured with a bag of marbles.
What is the difference in mass between:

1 the ball and the cup? ☐ marbles

2 the ball and the scissors? ☐ marbles

3 the cup and the scissors?  marbles

4 Would the ball be balanced if the cup and the scissors were placed in the other pan? ☐

UNIT 14

Number and Algebra

SET 1 Basic

1 4 + 4 = ☐

2 10 − 6 = ☐

3 8 + 3 = ☐

4 10 + 2 = ☐

5 5 + 1 = ☐

6 6 − 2 = ☐

7 Number after 7 = ☐

8 Number before 7 = ☐

9 Double 4 = ☐

10

Bree and Grant each bought 6 new games for their computer. How many do they have altogether?

☐

SET 2 Inverse operations

Write a subtraction fact from each addition fact.

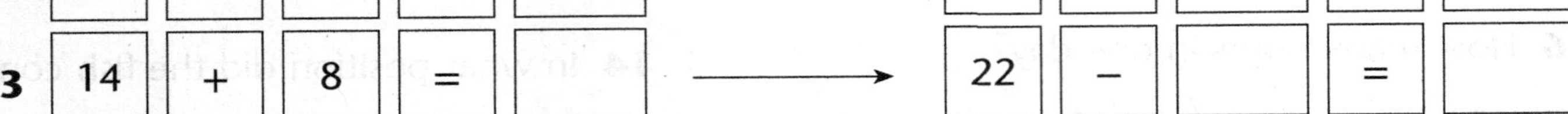

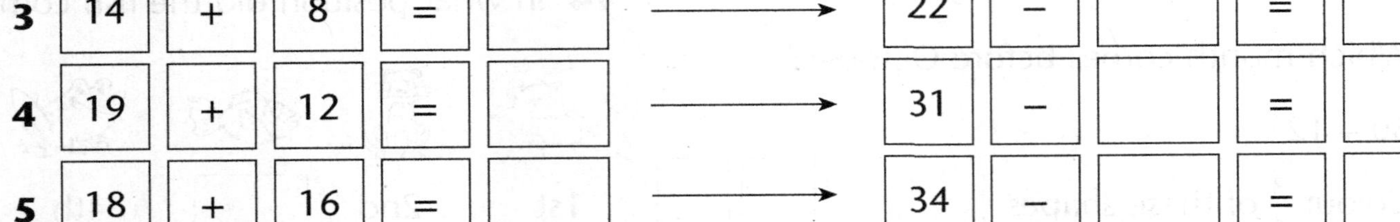

						→					
1	9	+	5	=	14	→	14	−		=	
2	8	+	7	=		→	15	−		=	
3	14	+	8	=		→	22	−		=	
4	19	+	12	=		→	31	−		=	
5	18	+	16	=		→	34	−		=	

Space Following directions

1 Go to the secret letter.

a Move up 2 spaces.

b Move right 5 spaces.

c Move up 3 spaces.

d Move right 2 spaces.

e Move up 1 space.

f Move left 5 spaces.

g Move down 2 spaces.

2 What letter did you find? ____________

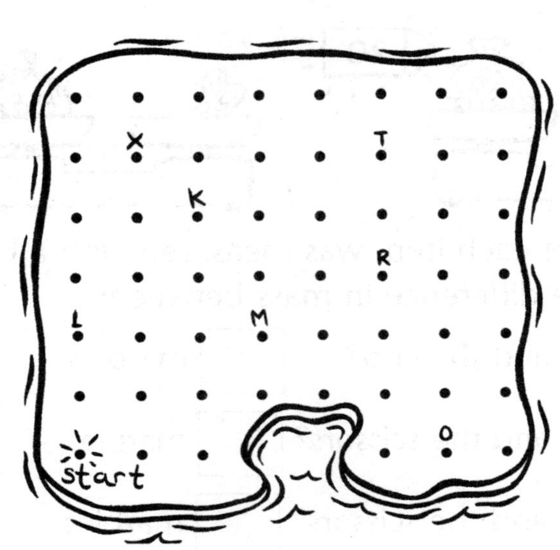

Number and Algebra

SET 3 Jump strategy for addition

Add the tens before the ones to complete the additions. The first one has been started.

1 34 + 25 becomes [34] + [20] + [5] = [ ]

2 33 + 14 becomes [ ] + [ ] + [ ] = [ ]

3 36 + 23 becomes [ ] + [ ] + [ ] = [ ]

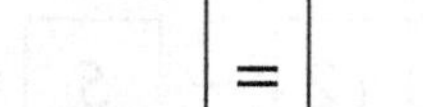

4 44 + 25 becomes [ ] + [ ] + [ ] = [ ]

5 55 + 32 becomes [ ] + [ ] + [ ] = [ ]

6

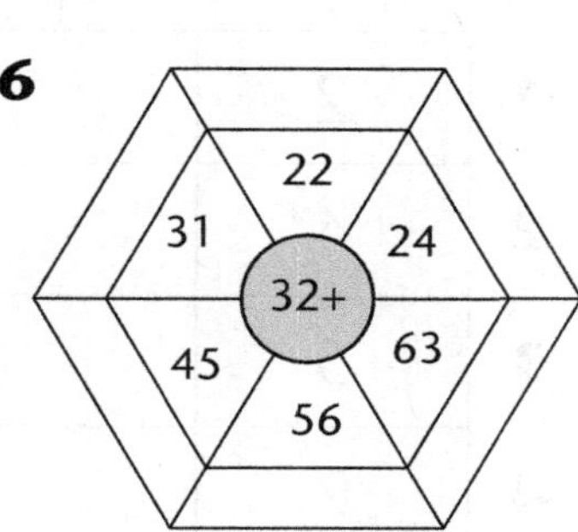

SET 4 Extension

1

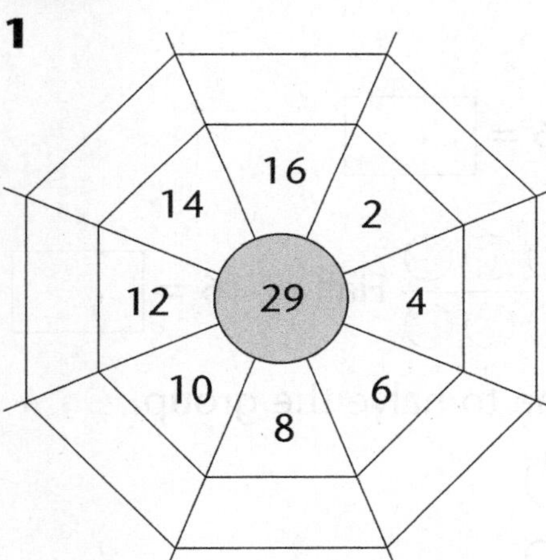

2 37 – 11 =

3 Is 21 odd or even?

4 Write three hundred and two.

5 [ ] + 13 = 80

6 Double 12.

7 5 × 4

8 39 + 21

9 How much is 3 dozen?

10 $5 – $1.50

11 98 = [ ] tens [ ] ones

12 Colour the heart that is 4 in from the left.

♡♡♡♡♡♡♡♡♡

Statistics and Probability Column graphs

Children's favourite colours

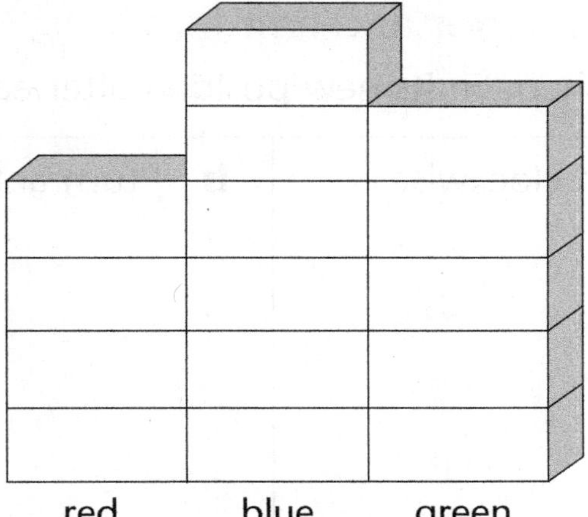

1 Which was the most favourite colour?

____

2 Which was the least favourite colour?

____

3 How many more children liked blue than green? ____________

4 How many children are represented in the graph? ____________

UNIT 15

Number and Algebra

SET 1 Basic

	+ 5	
1	2	
2	4	
3	5	
4	7	
5	10	
6	15	

7 6 + 3 = ☐

8 1 + 5 = ☐

9 12 − 5 = ☐

10

Luke owned 3 toy cars and his sister Lauren owned 3. How many cars did they own altogether?

☐

SET 2 Doubling and halving

1 3 + 3 = ☐

2 5 + 5 = ☐

3 6 + 6 = ☐

4 7 + 7 = ☐

5 8 + 8 = ☐

6 Half of 6 = ☐

7 Half of 16 = ☐

8 Draw a straight line to halve the group.

Space Quarter and half turns

Draw the shape in its new position after each turn.

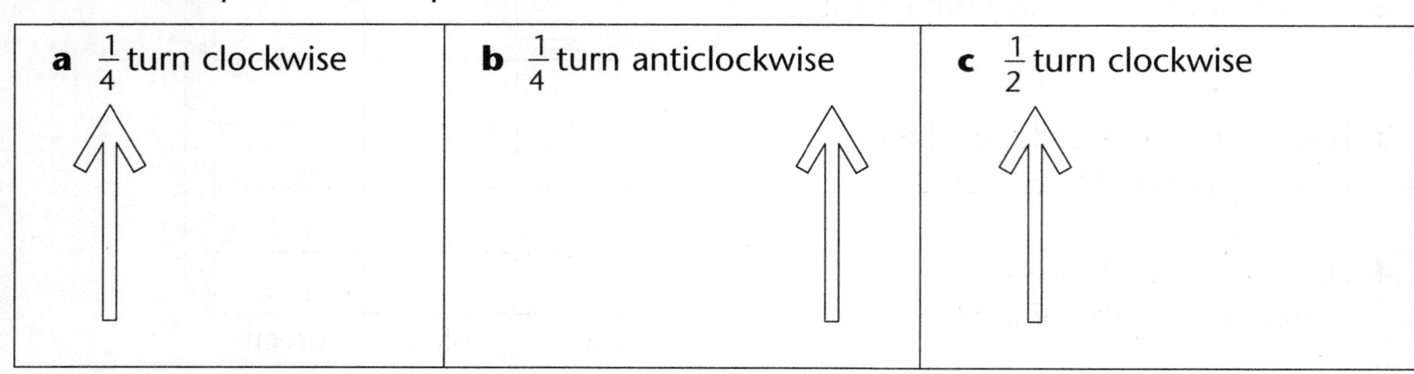

a $\frac{1}{4}$ turn clockwise

b $\frac{1}{4}$ turn anticlockwise

c $\frac{1}{2}$ turn clockwise

Number and Algebra

SET 3 Subtraction and addition

Complete the subtraction and addition number sentences.

1. 9 – 4 = ☐
2. 4 + 5 = ☐
3. 14 – 6 = ☐
4. 6 + ☐ = 14
5. 11 – 3 = ☐
6. 3 + ☐ = 11
7. 10 – 5 = ☐
8. 5 + ☐ = 10

SET 4 Extension

1. How many sides in 2 squares and 1 rectangle?
2. 22 + ☐ = 100
3. If Janice fell asleep at 9:00 pm and only slept for 3 hours, at what time did she wake up?
4. 5 + 12 + 6
5. Which season is the hottest?
6. 44 divided by 2
7. 15 lollies shared between 3 people ☐ lollies each.
8. 78 = ☐ tens ☐ ones
9. 50 – 12
10. 2 + 4 + 6
11. 9 groups of 2
12. $\frac{50}{100} = \frac{1}{}$
13. How many hours in 2 days?
14. Is 50 an odd or an even number?

Measurement Covering areas

Kim has started to cover these shapes with squares to measure their areas. Tick the largest shape and put a cross on the smallest shape.

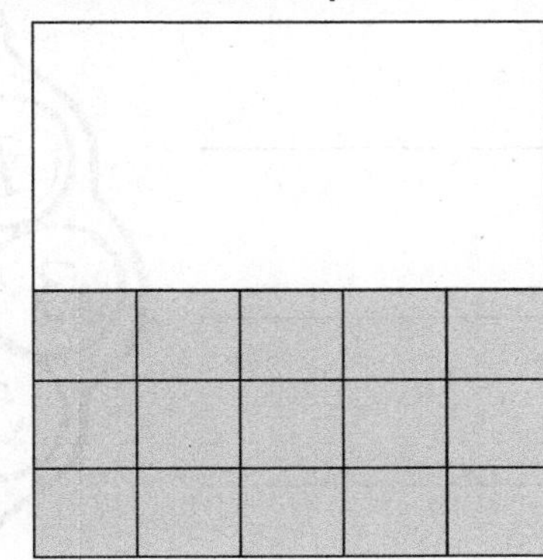

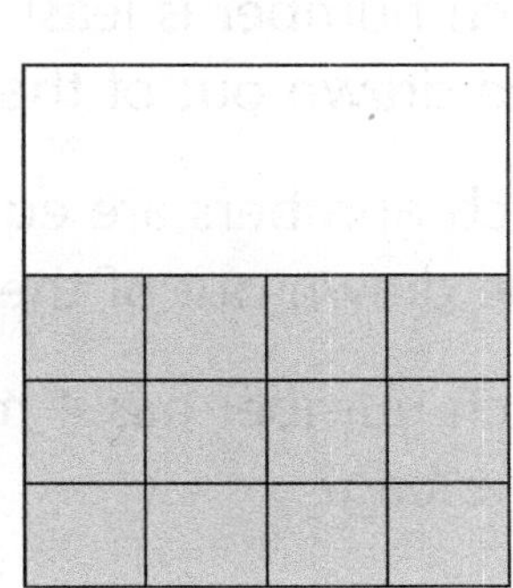

UNIT 16

Number and Algebra

SET 1 Basic

1 5 + 3 = ☐

2 4 − 2 = ☐

3 6 + 4 = ☐

4 8 + 5 = ☐

5 10 + 5 = ☐

6 15 − 5 = ☐

7 One more than 12 = ☐

8 Double 3 = ☐

9 One less than 6 = ☐

10

Jack's dad had 13 computers at his office. If 3 broke down, how many still work?

☐

SET 2 Recognising combinations and patterns

Complete these number combinations.

1

0	+ 4 =	4
	+ 3 =	4
	+ 2 =	4
	+ 1 =	4
	+ 0 =	4

2

0	+ 7 =	7
	+ 6 =	7
	+ 5 =	7
	+ 4 =	7
	+ 3 =	7
	+ 2 =	7
	+ 1 =	7
	+ 0 =	7

3

0	+ 10 =	10
	+ 9 =	10
	+ 8 =	10
	+ 7 =	10
	+ 6 =	10
	+ 5 =	10

	+ 4 =	10
	+ 3 =	10
	+ 2 =	10
	+ 1 =	10
	+ 0 =	10

Statistics and Probability Chance events

1 Which number is most likely to be drawn out of the bag? ______________

2 Which number is least likely to be drawn out of the bag? ______________

3 Which numbers are equally likely to be drawn out of the bag? ______________

4 Which number has 4 marbles in the bag? ______________

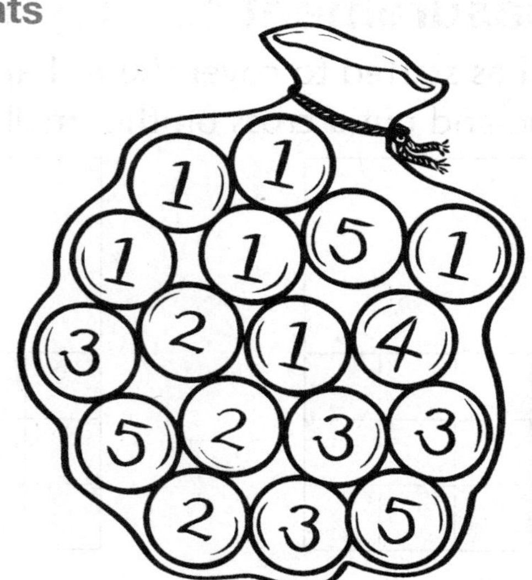

Number and Algebra

SET 3 Rounding to ten

Write the nearest 10 to each number.

1 9 ☐

2 22 ☐

3 25 ☐

4 48 ☐

5 61 ☐

Round these three-digit numbers to the nearest 10.

6 106 ☐

7 117 ☐

8 145 ☐

9 181 ☐

10 192 ☐

SET 4 Extension

1

+	1	2	3	4	10	11
9						

2 5 less than 80

3 How many days in a year?

4 How many legs on 3 cows?

5 10 + 3 + 13

6 How many months in 2 seasons?

7 ☐ – 20 = 120

8 20 divided by 2

9 25 + 25

10 How many sides on two triangles and three squares?

11 19 – 7

12 3 × 3

13 Write three hundred and thirty-five dollars.

Measurement Estimating with metres

Colour the correct box to describe the lengths.

	Length	Less than 1 metre	About 1 metre	More than 1 metre
1	The length of your desk			
2	The height of a door			
3	The width of your bedroom			
4	The height of your teacher			
5	The height of your desk			
6	Your height			

UNIT 17

Number and Algebra

SET 1 Basic

	−3	
1	3	
2	5	
3	6	
4	8	
5	10	
6	15	

7 7 + 3 = ☐

8 10 + 3 = ☐

9 18 − 3 = ☐

10 If 20 people try out for a play but there are only five parts, how many will miss out? ☐

SET 2 Repeated addition 2

Use the number line to help you complete the multiplications.

1 4 groups of 3 = ☐

2 4 groups of 4 = ☐

3 5 groups of 2 = ☐

4 3 groups of 5 = ☐

5 4 groups of 6 = ☐

6 5 groups of 5 = ☐

7 6 groups of 3 = ☐

8 7 groups of 4 = ☐

Space Describing objects

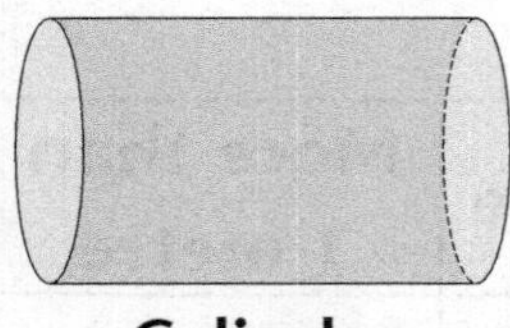

Cylinder

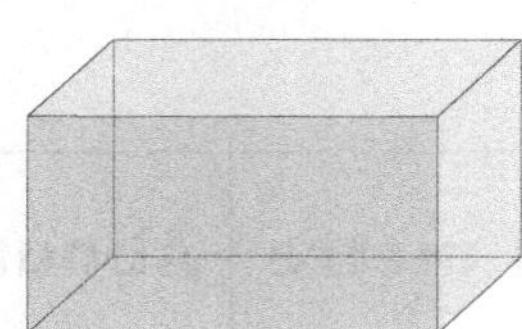

Prism

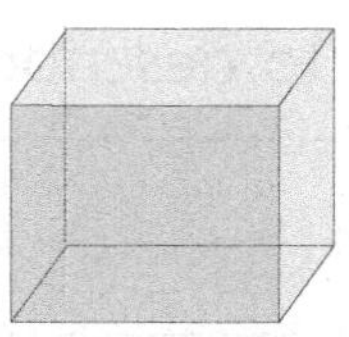

Cube

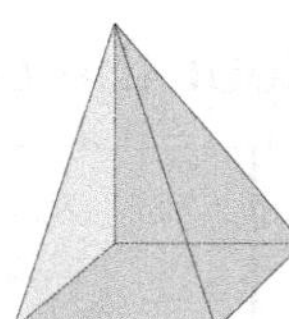

Pyramid

1 Which object above has 2 edges and 3 faces? ____________

2 Which object has 5 faces and 5 vertices? ____________

3 Which object has all its faces the same shape? ____________

4 Which objects have the same number of faces, edges and vertices?

____

Number and Algebra

SET 3 Recognising units of 100

Rocket Village 300 km
Mermaid Port 400 km
Pineapple Cove 700 km
Space Land 860 km
Banana Grove 1380 km

Use the signpost to answer the questions.

How many units of 100 is it to:

1 Rocket Village? ________

2 Mermaid Port? ________

3 Pineapple Cove? ________

Which place is closest to:

4 9 units of 100? ____________________

5 14 units of 100? ____________________

SET 4 Extension

1 9 + 3 + 2

2 48 hours = ☐ days

3 15c + 20c + $1

4 2 × 7

5 Total of 15 and 7

6 300, 400, ☐, 600, ☐

7 Subtract 20c from $2.

8 $5 – $2.50

9 2 tens plus 3 ones

10 46 to the nearest 10

11 8, ☐, 4, 2

12 What is the sum of three and ten?

13 Colour the heart that is two in from the left red, and the heart four in from the right blue.

Measurement Quarter to and quarter past

Record the time below each clock.

1

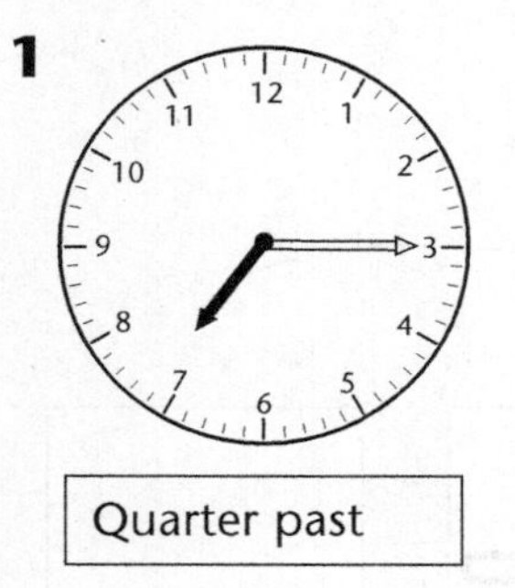

Quarter past

2

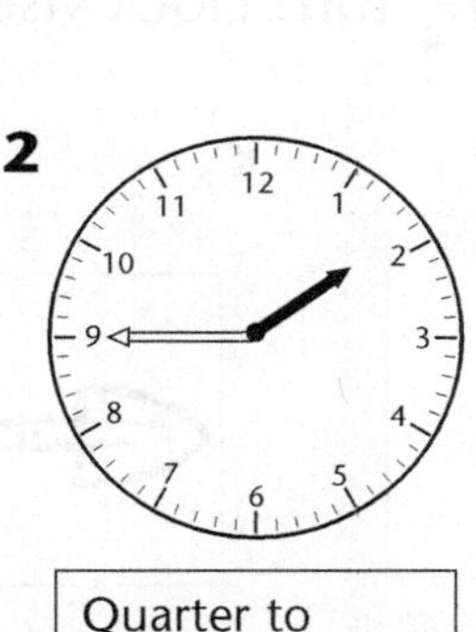

Quarter to

3

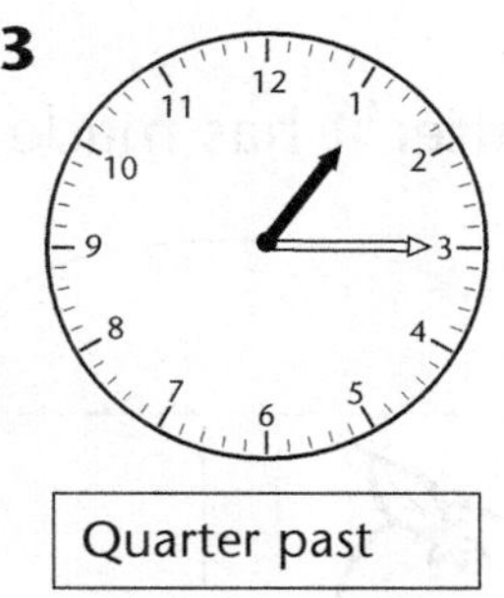

Quarter past

4

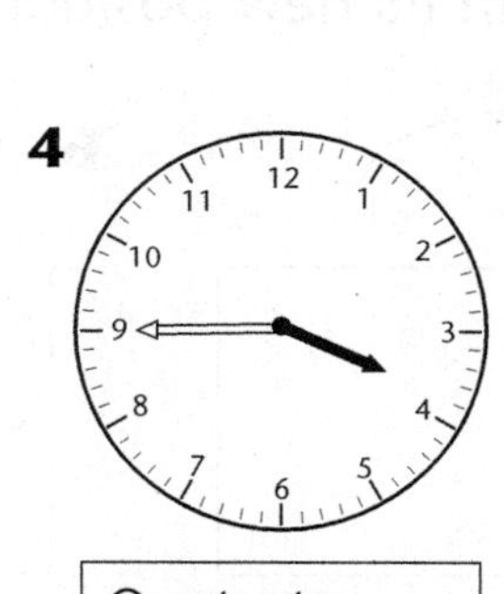

Quarter to

5

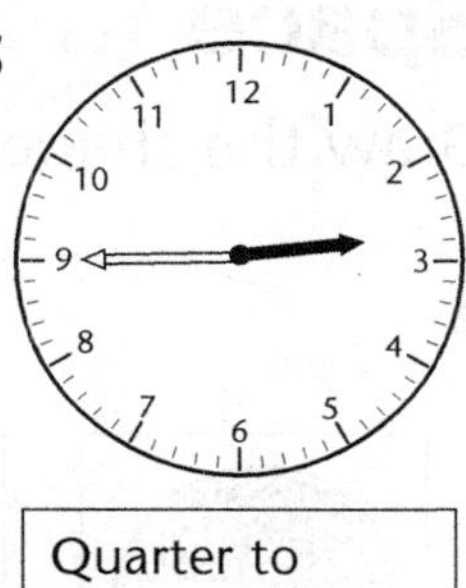

Quarter to

Number and Algebra

SET 1 Basic

1 7 − 1 = ☐

2 3 + 3 = ☐

3 4 + 3 = ☐

4 10 − 5 = ☐

5 8 − 3 = ☐

6 6 + 4 = ☐

7 One more than 11 = ☐

8 Is 18 an odd number? ☐

9 2 × 4 = ☐

10

If there are 16 pages in a book and Phil has read 3, how many are left? ☐

SET 2 Equal rows and columns

Use the term "rows of" to complete the multiplications.

1 2 rows of 5 = ☐

2 ☐ rows of ☐ = ☐

3 ☐ rows of ☐ = ☐

4 ☐ rows of ☐ = ☐

Space Turns

Draw the shape in its new position after it has made a $\frac{1}{4}$ turn clockwise.

a

b

c

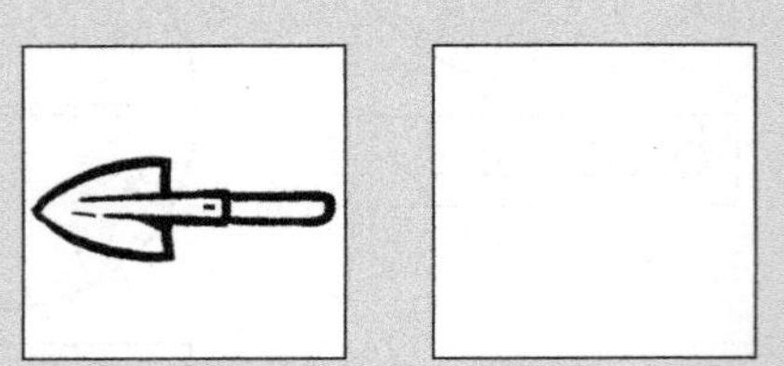

Number and Algebra

SET 3 Halves, quarters and eighths

Use the models to find the fractions of the groups.

1

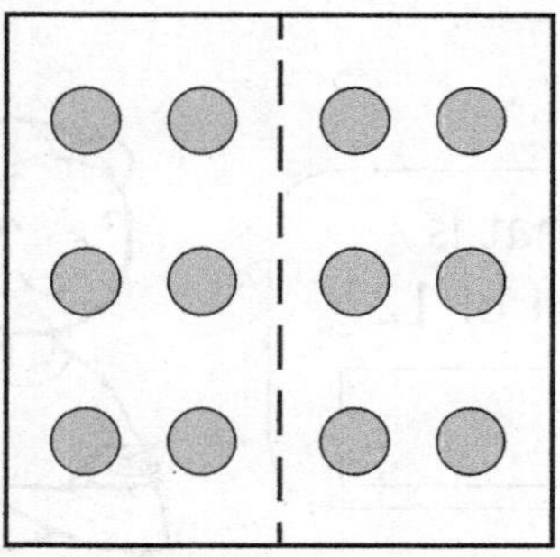

How many circles in half the group? ☐

2

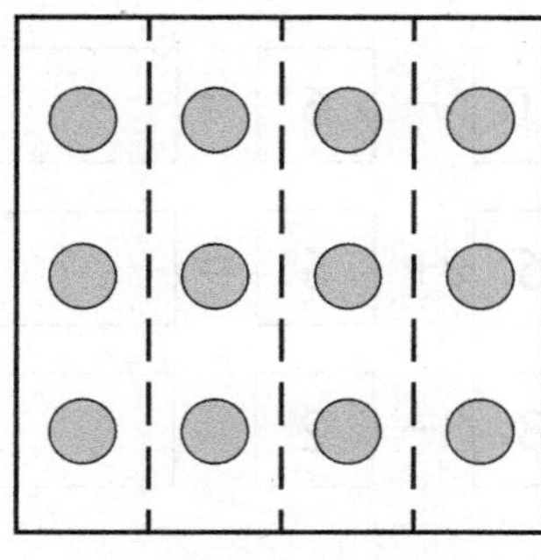

How many circles in one quarter of the group? ☐

3

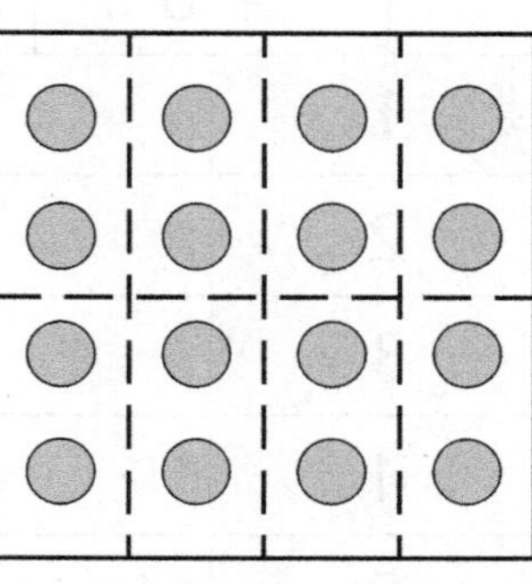

How many circles in one eighth of the group? ☐

SET 4 Extension

1 Is 26 odd or even?

2 28 + ☐ = 35

3 7 less than 9

4 7 more than 9

5 6 + 3 + 2

6 22 + 26

7 Four thirty in digital time

8 How much are 3 envelopes at 50c each?

9 95 = ☐ tens ☐ ones

10 Total of 30 and 300

11 Which day follows Sunday?

12 Which is greater: 2 dozen or 21?

13 Round 42 to the nearest 10.

Measurement Area

Colour the bigger shape in each pair.

1

2

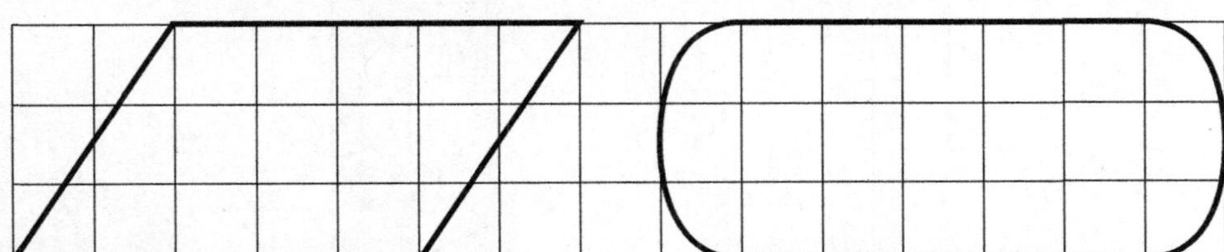

Number and Algebra

SET 1 Basic

	+ 6	
1	1	
2	2	
3	3	
4	4	
5	5	
6	10	

7 10 − 6 = ☐

8 6 + 6 = ☐

9 8 − 2 = ☐

10

What is half of 12? ☐

SET 2 Doubles and near doubles

1 3 + 3 = ☐

2 5 + 5 = ☐

3 6 + 6 = ☐

4 7 + 8 = ☐

5 8 + 9 = ☐

6 30 + 30 = ☐

7 50 + 50 = ☐

8 60 + 60 = ☐

9 70 + 80 = ☐

10 80 + 90 = ☐

11 Will put $40 in the bank on Monday and $40 on Tuesday. How much did he put in the bank? ☐ + ☐ = ☐

Space Symmetry

Complete the symmetrical shapes.

1

2

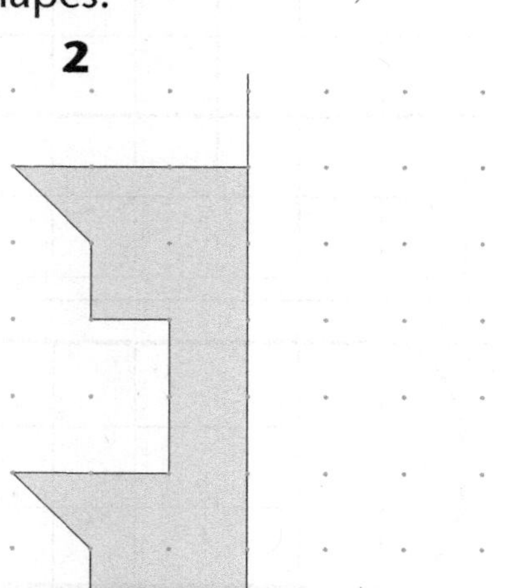

3

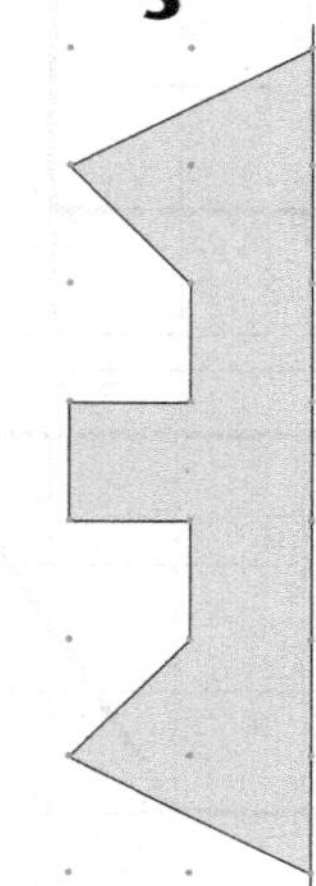

Number and Algebra

SET 3 Rows and columns

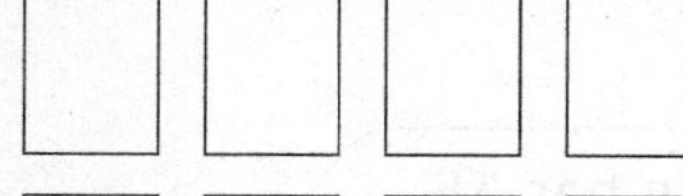
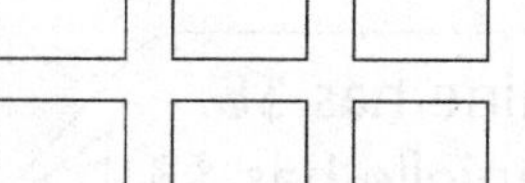

1 How many rows of 4 are there in 8? ☐

2 How many columns of 2 are there in 8? ☐

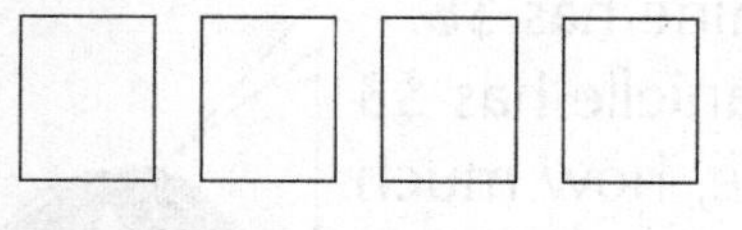

3 How many rows of 4 are there in 12? ☐

4 How many columns of 3 are there in 12? ☐

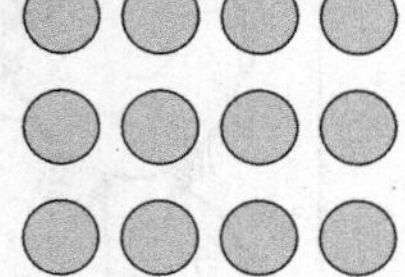

5 How many rows of 7 are there in 21? ☐

6 How many columns of 3 are there in 21? ☐

SET 4 Extension

1 What is the sum of 3 + 4 + 10?

2 Write the largest 3-digit number you can using 7, 9, 2.

3 36 + 4 tens

4 $1.50 + $3

5 Write the smallest 3-digit number you can using 3, 4, 1.

6 ☐ tens + 3 ones = 73

7 $\frac{1}{2}$ of 6

8 10, 20, 30, 40, 50
Rule: ____________________

9 25 + 75

10 ☐ + 3 = 100

11 Add 30 to 47.

12 What is the product of two and three?

13

–	10	13	16	19	20	50
3						

Measurement Comparing mass

Draw something in the other pan which is heavier than the apple.

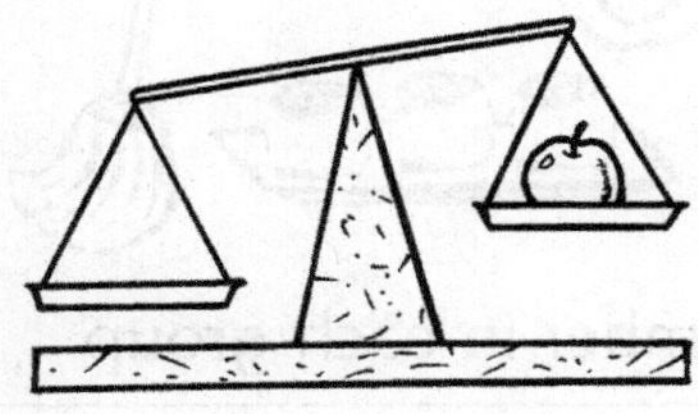

____________________ is heavier than an apple.

UNIT
20

Number and Algebra

SET 1 Basic

1. 4 − 4 = ☐
2. 6 + 4 = ☐
3. 5 − 2 = ☐
4. 12 + 5 = ☐
5. 15 − 5 = ☐
6. 17 − 2 = ☐
7. 5 less than 15 = ☐
8. One less than 13 = ☐
9. 3 × 3 = ☐
10. Jasmine has $8. If Danielle has $3 more, how much does Danielle have? ☐

SET 2 Arrays of two

Complete the number sentences to describe the arrays.

1 2 3 4 5

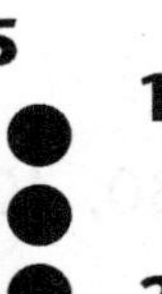
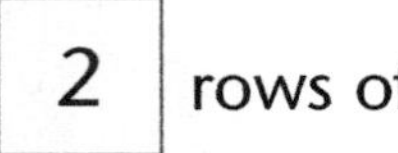
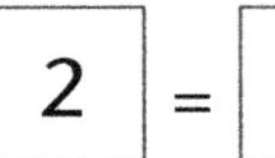
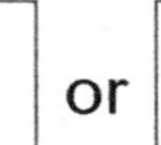
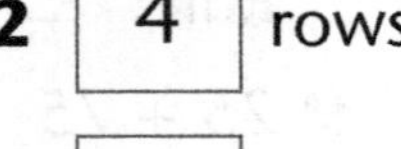
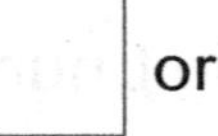

1. 2 rows of 2 = ☐ or 2 × 2 = ☐
2. 4 rows of 2 = ☐ or 4 × 2 = ☐
3. 5 rows of 2 = ☐ or 5 × 2 = ☐
4. 6 rows of 2 = ☐ or 6 × 2 = ☐
5. 8 rows of 2 = ☐ or 8 × 2 = ☐

Statistics and Probability Gather and compare data

Make two more categories or groups of things, then tally the number in each group.

Cleaning materials 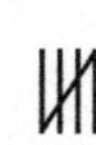		

Number and Algebra

SET 3 Rounding to 10

Round each number to the nearest 10.

1 19 ______	**4** 22 ______	**7** 92 ______	**10** 45 ______
2 29 ______	**5** 38 ______	**8** 43 ______	**11** 57 ______
3 31 ______	**6** 51 ______	**9** 49 ______	**12** 69 ______

Estimate an answer by rounding all numbers to the nearest 10.

13 [19] + [22] ≈ [ ]

14 [33] + [21] ≈ [ ]

15 [29] + [18] ≈ [ ]

16 [27] + [32] ≈ [ ]

17 [33] + [48] ≈ [ ]

18 [28] + [43] ≈ [ ]

SET 4 Extension

1 7 + 8 + 7

2 Cost of a $10 cake and a $3 tart

3 How many days in 3 weeks?

4 16 ÷ 2

5 90, 100, 110, [ ], 130

Rule: ______________________

6 36 + 20

7 How many days in a school week?

8 How many months in 2 years?

9 50 − 5 − 5

10 Write the smallest number you can using 7, 6, 8.

11 Write the largest number you can using 7, 6, 8.

12 a

	Tens	Ones
	1	5
+	1	7

b

	Tens	Ones
	1	2
+	2	9

Measurement Metres and half metres

1 Put a ● on the rope to show where half a metre is.

0 — 1 metre

2 Put a ● on the rope to show where one and a half metres is.

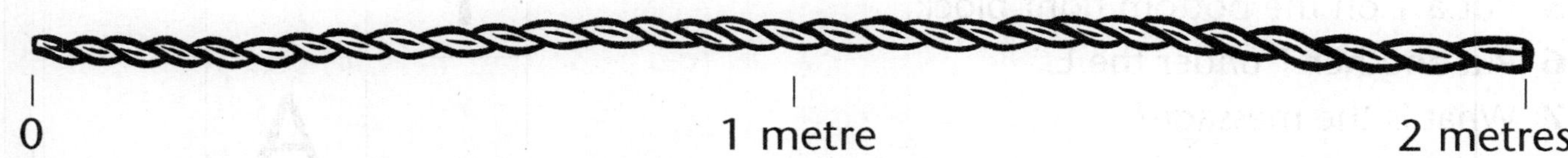

0 — 1 metre — 2 metres

Number and Algebra

SET 1 Basic

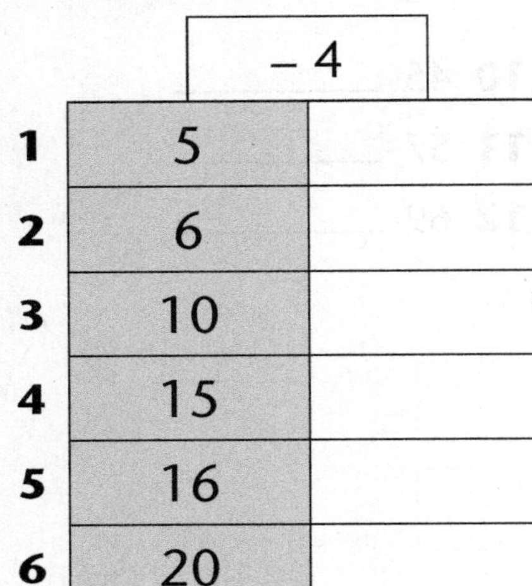

	−4	
1	5	
2	6	
3	10	
4	15	
5	16	
6	20	

7 12 − 2 = ☐

8 14 − 4 = ☐

9 10 + 4 = ☐

10

Jana had $15 but spent $4 on a book. How much does she have left? ☐

SET 2 Constant difference

Supply another number sentence to balance the beams.

1 8 + 6 | 4 + ☐

2 9 + 8 | 6 + ☐

3 9 + 6 | 3 + ☐

4 20 − 4 | 18 − ☐

5 11 − 7 | 15 − ☐

6 18 − 5 | 15 − ☐

Space Sketching position

Petri built a model out of blocks. Put the letters on the blocks to discover the secret message.

1 Put an O on the top left block.

2 Put an A on the middle block.

3 Put a C on the bottom left block.

4 Put an E on the top right block.

5 Put a T on the bottom right block.

6 Put another T under the E.

7 What is the message?

____

Number and Algebra

SET 3 Rounding to 100

Round each number to the nearest 100.

1 291 ≈ ______ 3 320 ≈ ______ 5 505 ≈ ______

2 375 ≈ ______ 4 595 ≈ ______ 6 385 ≈ ______

270 is almost 300.

Round each number to the nearest 100 to make adding easier.

				≈	
7	199	+	199	≈	
8	98	+	295	≈	
9	303	+	199	≈	
10	196	+	108	≈	
11	497	+	215	≈	
12	509	+	196	≈	

SET 4 Extension

1

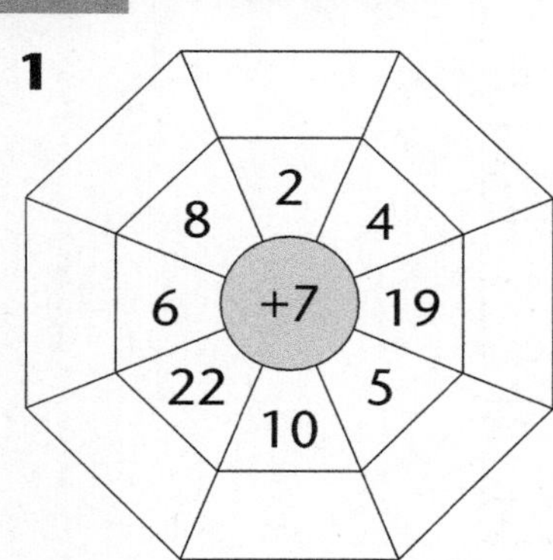

2 250c = $ ☐.☐☐

3 30 + 30 + 30

4 How many 10c pieces are in $1?

5 Is 72 odd or even?

6 13, 15, ____, 19, 21, ____

7 21 × 0

8 How many groups of 5 can be made from 20 marbles?

9 What is the possibility of snow today?

10 Make up 3 number sentences that equal 12.

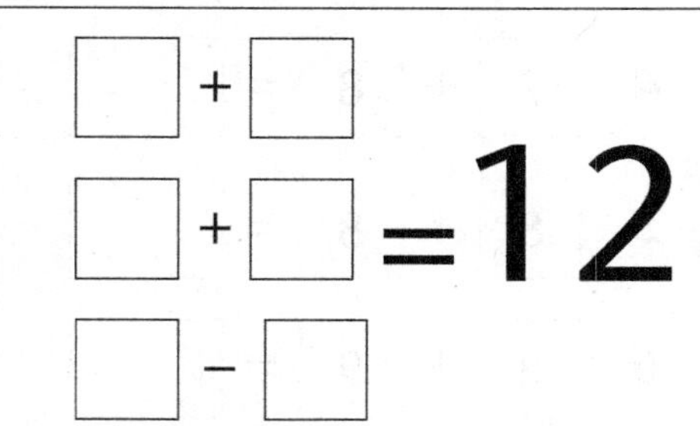

Measurement Digital time

Draw a line to match each clock face to a digital time.

	3	:	3	0
	6	:	0	0
	8	:	0	0
	5	:	0	0
	2	:	3	0
1	0	:	3	0

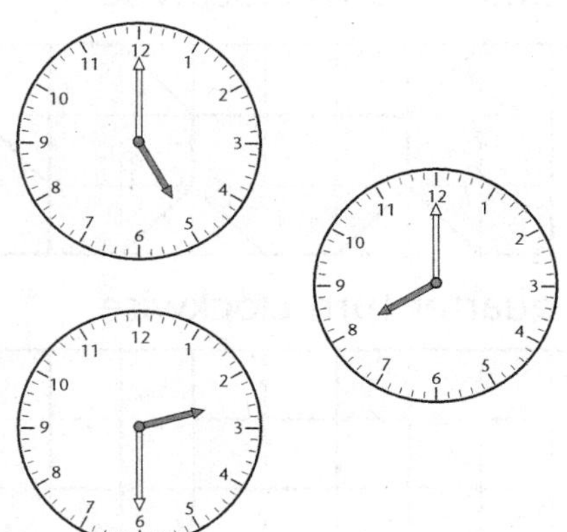

UNIT 22

Number and Algebra

SET 1 Basic

1 10 − 5 = ☐

2 3 + 2 = ☐

3 5 − 1 = ☐

4 8 + 3 = ☐

5 14 + 5 = ☐

6 6 − 4 = ☐

7 Double 5 = ☐

8 One more than 19 = ☐

9 Is 10 an even number?

☐

10

John had a pack of 20 stamps but used 3 to send a parcel. How many does he have left?

☐

SET 2 Extending addition facts

Complete these sets of related addition facts.

1	6 + 6 = ☐	60 + 60 = ☐
2	6 + 7 = ☐	60 + 70 = ☐
3	7 + 7 = ☐	70 + 70 = ☐
4	7 + 8 = ☐	70 + 80 = ☐
5	8 + 8 = ☐	80 + 80 = ☐
6	8 + 9 = ☐	80 + 90 = ☐

Space Turning patterns

Continue the turning patterns.

1 quarter turn clockwise

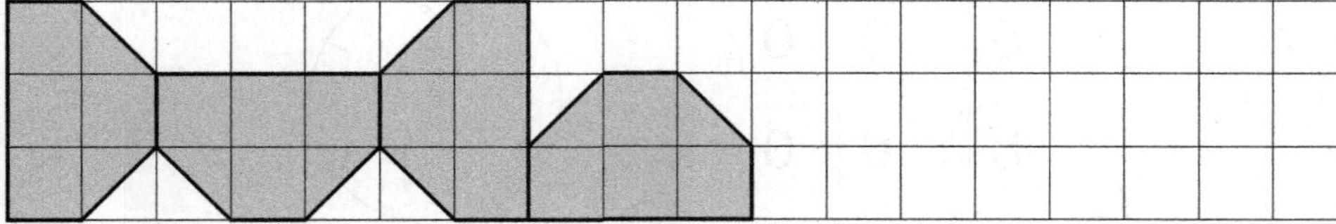

2 quarter turn clockwise

Number and Algebra

SET 3 Representing 3-digit numbers

Record the number represented by each numeral expander.

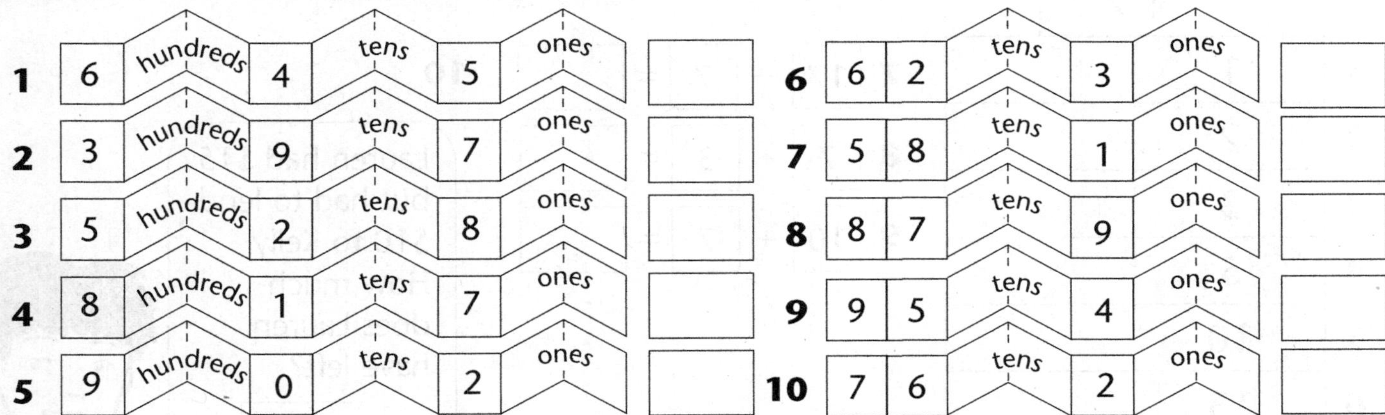

SET 4 Extension

1 ☐ + 7 = 25

2 9 + 4 + 6

3 Half of 40

4 $10 – 50c

5 Round 53 to the nearest 10.

6 How many legs do 4 cows have?

7 What is the value of 7 in 374?

8 ☐ × 10 = 20

9 How many 5c pieces in 30c?

10 How many halves in 2 wholes?

11 On the diagram below, label Jasmine in 3rd place, Kelly in 5th and Kristy in 7th.

Statistics and Probability Picture graphs

Amy recorded the hair colours of the children in her class.
Make a picture graph by drawing a ☺ for each tally mark in the table.

red							
brown							
fair							
black							
blonde							

Colour	Tally
red	IIII
brown	𝍸 III
fair	𝍸
black	𝍸 I
blonde	III

Number and Algebra

SET 1 Basic

		+ 7
1	1	
2	2	
3	3	
4	5	
5	10	
6	13	

7 17 − 7 = ☐

8 7 + 3 = ☐

9 10 + 7 = ☐

10

Lauren had $15 but had to lend $10 to Kelly. How much does Lauren have left?

☐

SET 2 Extending subtraction facts

Complete these sets of related subtractions.

1 5 − 3 = ☐ 50 − 30 = ☐

2 7 − 5 = ☐ 70 − 50 = ☐

3 9 − 4 = ☐ 90 − 40 = ☐

4 10 − 7 = ☐ 100 − 70 = ☐

5 There were 12 cakes but Susan ate 3 of them. How many are left?

☐ − ☐ = ☐

6 There were 120 people but 30 left early. How many are still there?

☐ − ☐ = ☐

Space Prisms

Draw a line to match each description to a prism.

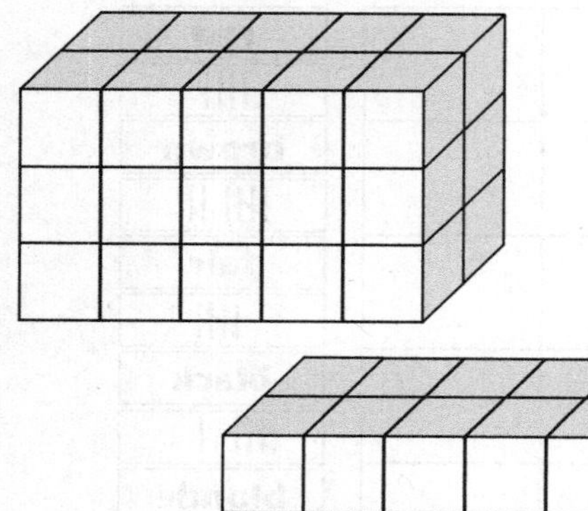

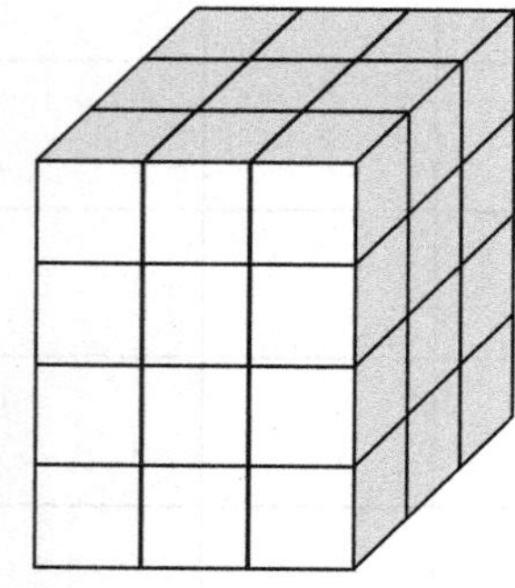

I am 5 blocks in length with a width of 2 and a height of 2.

I am 3 blocks in length with a width of 3 and a height of 4.

I am 5 blocks in length with a width of 2 and a height of 3.

Number and Algebra

SET 3 Commutative property

Write two number sentences to describe each picture.

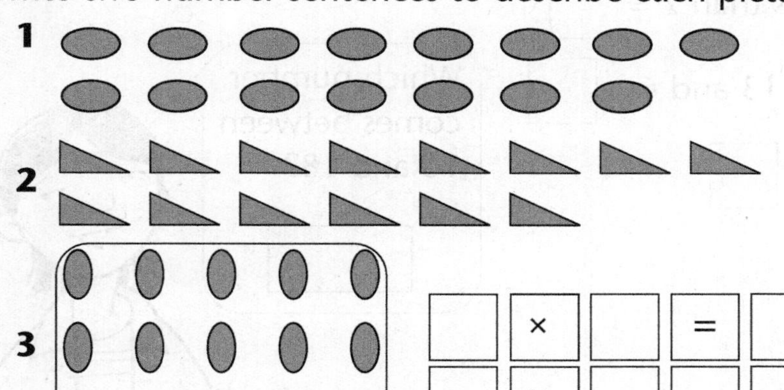

1

8	+		=	15
	+	8	=	15

2

	+		=	
	+		=	

3

	×		=	
	×		=	

SET 4 Extension

1 Which is bigger: $\frac{1}{3}$ or $\frac{1}{2}$?

2 How many weeks in a year?

3 10 + 6 + 5

4 ☐ − 4 = 44

5 How many 50c cakes can I buy with $2.50?

6 18 plus 6

7 How many months in 2 years?

8 How many days in 3 school weeks?

9 If the big hand is on the 12 and the small hand is on the 3, what is the time?

10 125c = $ ____ _ ____ ____

11 $5.50 take away 25c

12 What is the total number of sides for this group of shapes?

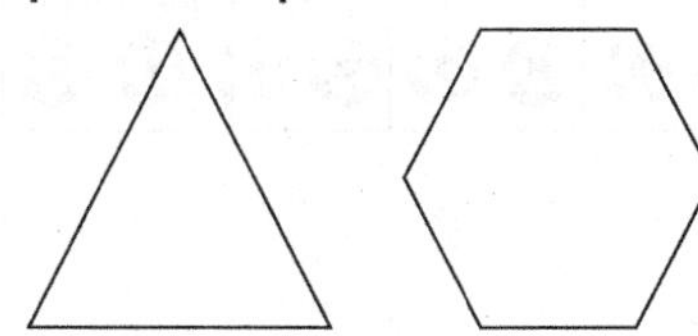

Measurement Halves, quarters and eighths

1 Put a cross on the item that is one quarter the length of the javelin.

2 Circle the item that is one half the length of the javelin.

3 Tick the item that is one eighth the length of the javelin.

UNIT
24

Number and Algebra

SET 1 Basic

1 14 − 4 = ☐

2 10 − 6 = ☐

3 4 + 4 = ☐

4 16 − 6 = ☐

5 20 − 5 = ☐

6 10 + 8 = ☐

7 Two less than 7 = ☐

8 Sum of 13 and 6 = ☐

9 2 × 7 = ☐

10

SET 2 Halves, quarters and eighths

Whole	16 balls
Halves	8 balls | 8 balls
Quarters	4 | 4 | 4 | 4 balls
Eighths	2 | 2 | 2 | 2 | 2 | 2 | 2 | 2 balls

There are 16 balls in the whole group.

1 How many balls are in one half of the group? ☐

2 How many balls are in one quarter of the group? ☐

3 How many balls are in one eighth of the group? ☐

Measurement The calendar

February				
Sunday	1	8	15	22
Monday	2	9	16	23
Tuesday	3	10	17	24
Wednesday	4	11	18	25
Thursday	5	12	19	26
Friday	6	13	20	27
Saturday	7	14	21	28

1 How many days are there in this month on the calendar? ______

2 What day is February 5? ______

3 What day is 3 days after February 12? ______

4 What is the date of the third Friday in February? ______

5 Name the day and date 1 week after February 16. ______

Number and Algebra

SET 3 Number problems

1 There are 12 birds in a tree. If 7 more joined them, how many would there be?

2 Jack has three money boxes. One has \$7, one has \$8 and one has \$3. How much has he got altogether?

3 20 birds were in the tree but 12 flew away. How many are still in the tree?

4 Bree has 2 dozen eggs but broke 10 of them. How many are left?

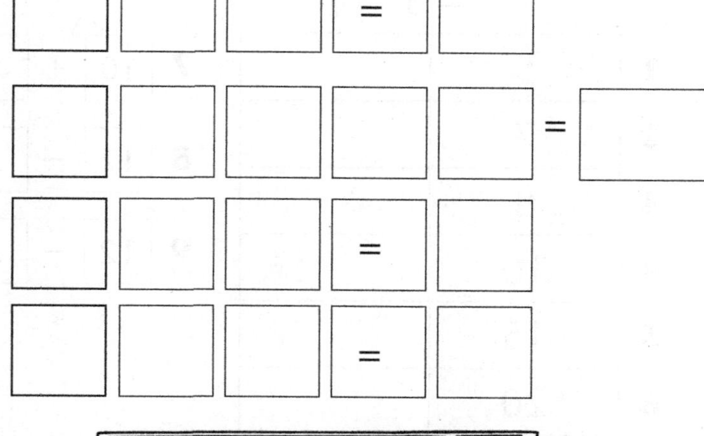

5 Write a number sentence to describe what has happened to the full tray of cakes.

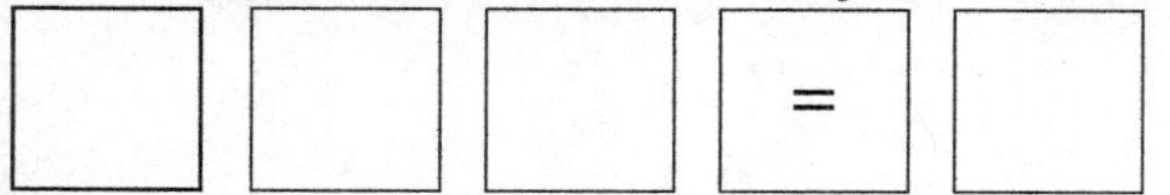

SET 4 Extension

1 6 + 4 + 6

2 How many seconds in one minute?

3 Cost of a \$3 cake and a \$4 tart

4
```
  $ 1 . 5 0
+   1 . 2 5
-----------
```

5
```
  $ 2 . 2 5
+   1 . 7 5
-----------
```

6 One train ticket is 25c. How much for 3?

7 Nine divided by three

8 Which is larger: 1 kg or 100 g?

9 How many minutes in one hour?

10 65 + 25

11 ☐ divided by 4 = 5

12 What is the value of the 9 in 393?

13 7 + ☐ = 13

14 How many legs do 3 cats have?

Measurement Volume of objects

How many blocks make up the volume of these solid prisms?

1 2 3 4

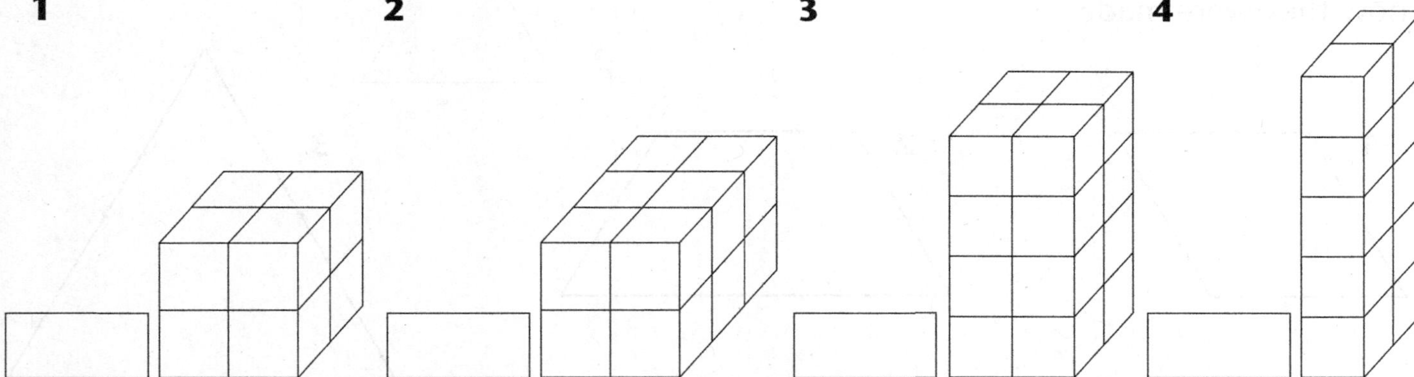

Number and Algebra

SET 1 Basic

	−5	
1	5	
2	7	
3	8	
4	10	
5	15	
6	20	

7 10 + 5 = ☐

8 17 − 5 = ☐

9 12 − 5 = ☐

10 If Alicia lost 5 marbles out of her packet of 17, how many does she have left? ☐

SET 2 Shopkeeper's method

Calculate how much has to be added on to the smaller number to complete the subtractions.

1 90 − 76 think 76 + ☐ + ☐ = ☐

2 70 − 53 think 53 + ☐ + ☐ = ☐

3 50 − 32 think 32 + ☐ + ☐ = ☐

4 60 − 49 think 49 + ☐ + ☐ = ☐

Space Combining shapes

The shaded triangle was used to make the shapes below. Draw dotted lines on the shapes to show how they were made.

1 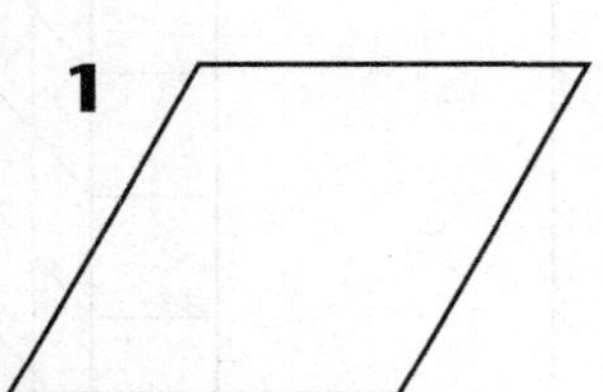

2 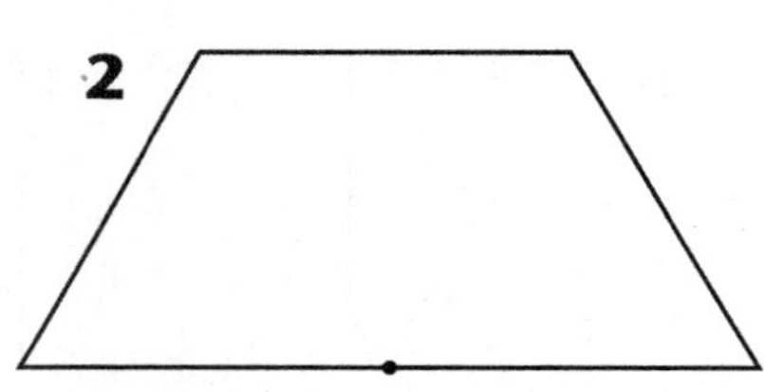

3 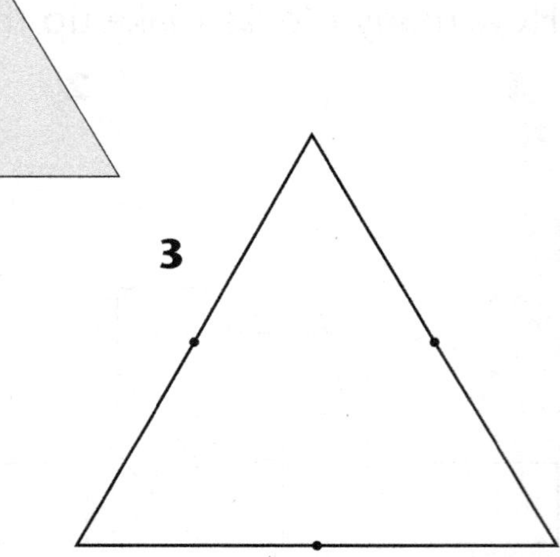

Number and Algebra

SET 3 Number bond combinations to 20

Complete the number bonds.

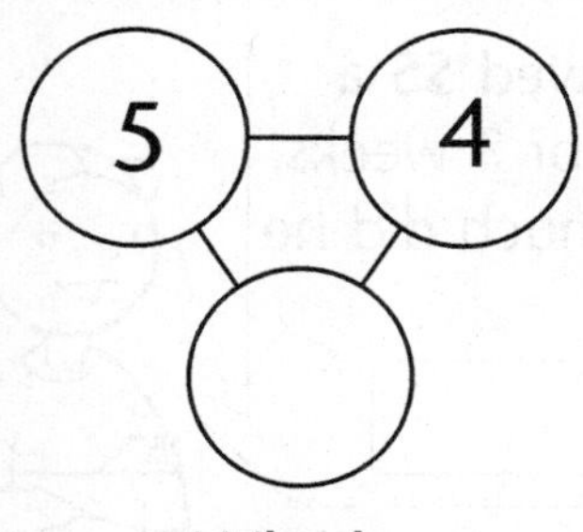

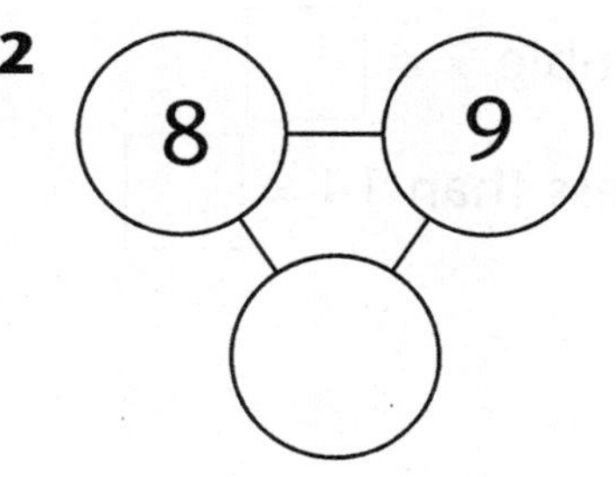

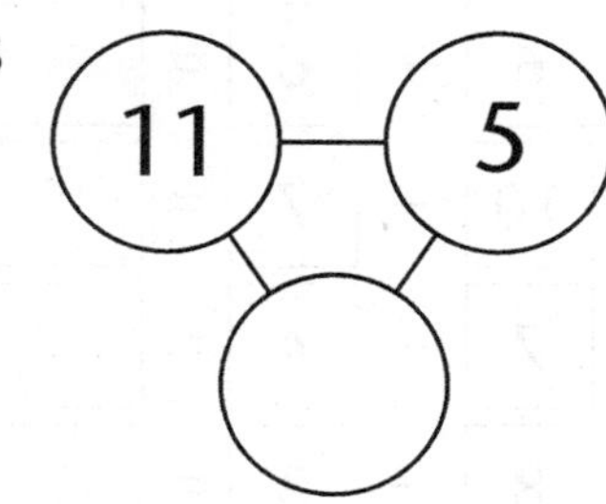

Use number bonds to find the whole.

4	4 + 3		5 + 2		6 + 1	
5	8 + 5		10 + 3		11 + 2	

SET 4 Extension

1 Write 29 in words.

____

2 How many minutes in half an hour?

3 2 + 7 + 8 =

4 25 – 7

5 What are two shapes that have 4 sides?

6 How many days in 3 weeks?

7 18 + ☐ = 30

8 Which is heavier: 2 kg of feathers or 1 kg of lead?

9 How much are two combs at $2.50 each?

10 Value of 8 in 3086?

11 Draw a pattern of a square, then a triangle, then a pentagon, then a circle.

Measurement Time/seasons

List the months that belong to each season. It has been started for you.

Summer	Spring	Winter	Autumn
December			

UNIT 26

Number and Algebra

SET 1 Basic

1 10 + 6 = ☐

2 6 + 6 = ☐

3 10 − 7 = ☐

4 7 + 4 = ☐

5 8 − 3 = ☐

6 4 − 2 = ☐

7 $7 + $3= ☐

8 Double 9 = ☐

9 7 less than 14 = ☐

10

Billy saved $5 a week for 3 weeks. How much did he save? ☐

SET 2 Subtracting tens before the ones

1 26 − 13 = ☐

2 28 − 12 = ☐

3 34 − 13 = ☐

4 36 − 21 = ☐

5 38 − 23 = ☐

6 46 − 22 = ☐

7 47 − 23 = ☐

8 48 − 21 = ☐

9 36 − 23 = ☐

10 45 − 22 = ☐

Statistics and Probability Posing questions

Favourite sports in my class

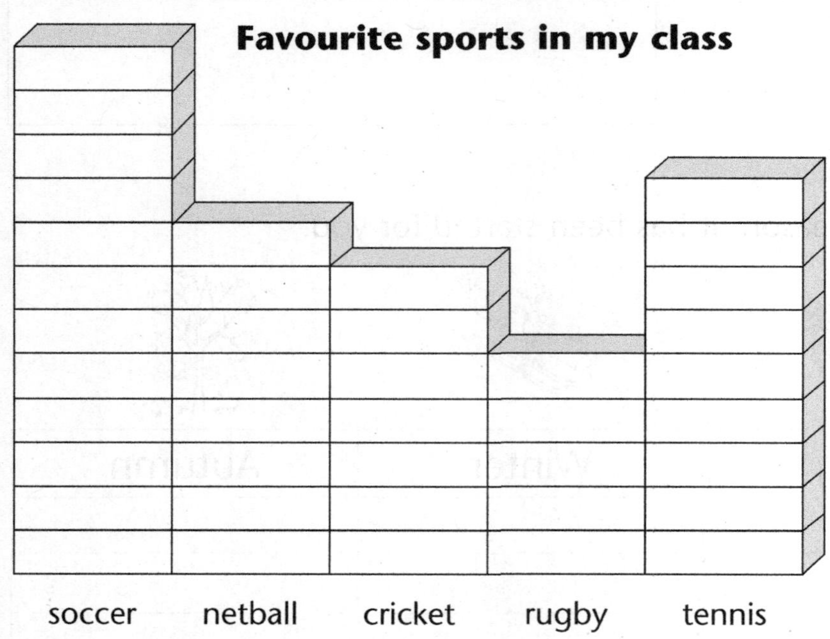

1 How many children like soccer best? ____________

2 How many children like cricket best? ____________

3 How many children like netball best? ____________

4 Write a question about the graph.

____

____

Number and Algebra

SET 3 Halves and quarters of a group

Colour half of each collection.

1  

2    

Colour a quarter of each collection.

3    

4     

SET 4 Extension

1 $\frac{1}{4}$ of 40

2 How many legs on one spider?

3 How many legs on three spiders?

4 2 × ☐ = 40

5 Share $100 among four people.

6 How many days in a leap year?

7 13, 15, 17, ____, 21

8 21 + 12 + 9

9 What number comes after 99?

10 Is 99 odd or even?

11 There are 30 people in Kaia's class but 7 are away today. How many people are there today?

12 How much money is there below?

$____ . ____ ____

Measurement Centimetres

Use a ruler to measure the length of each pencil in centimetres.

1 Jack ☐ cm

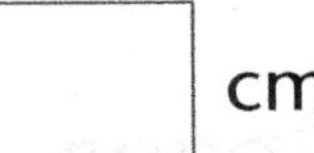

2  Malak 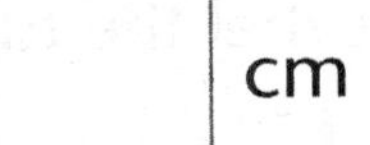 cm

3  Henri 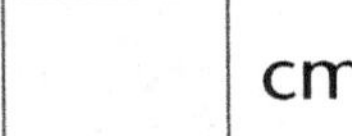 cm

4 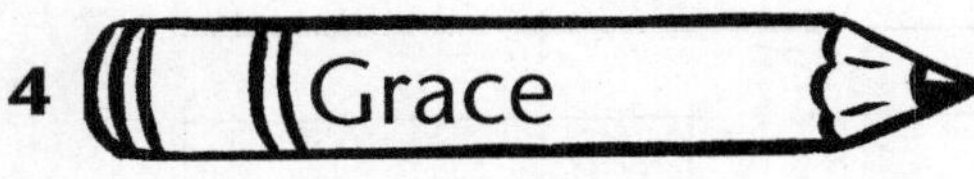 Grace 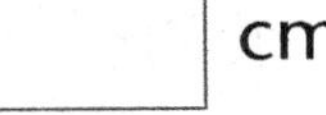 cm

5  Mustafa  cm

Number and Algebra

SET 1 Basic

		+ 8
1	1	
2	2	
3	5	
4	7	
5	10	
6	11	

7 20 − 8 = ☐

8 12 + 8 = ☐

9 6 + 8 = ☐

10

SET 2 Multiplication (×5)

Write the answer for each balloon on its basket.

1 

2 

3 

4 

5 

6 

7 

8 

Space Full, quarter and half turns

Label the turns as half, full or quarter.

1

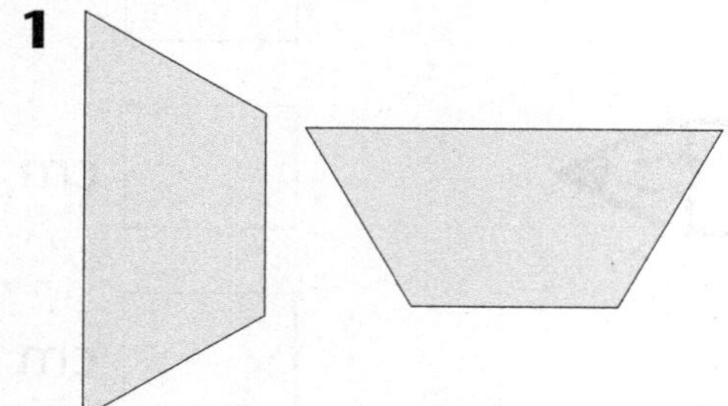

2

3

Number and Algebra

SET 3 Multiplication using repeated addition

Solve the multiplications using repeated addition.

1 There were three teams with five players in each team. How many players were there in total?

☐ + ☐ + ☐ = ☐

2 There were four packets of biscuits with four biscuits in each packet. How many biscuits were there altogether?

☐ + ☐ + ☐ + ☐ = ☐

SET 4 Extension

1 4 + 4 + 4

2 $\frac{1}{4}$ = ☐ %

3 $\frac{1}{2}$ = ☐ %

4 7 tens plus 13 ones

5 Which number sentence has the answer 21?

○ 15 + 8
○ 30 − 8
○ 3 × 6
○ 3 × 7

6 Mia is 5 and Jenna is twice her age. How old is Jenna?

7 8 + ☐ = 13

8 If two drinks cost $4, how much would one be?

9 5 into 25 goes ☐ times.

10 How many grams in a kilogram?

11 Round 293 to the nearest 100.

12 Half of 90

Measurement Area

Calculate the total area of each shape by counting the squares.

1

☐ squares

2

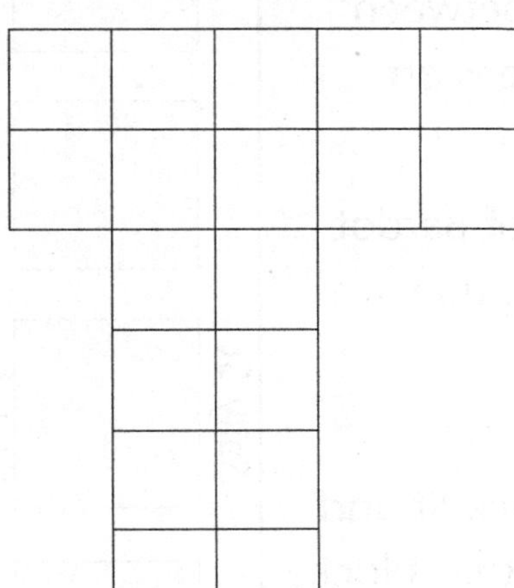

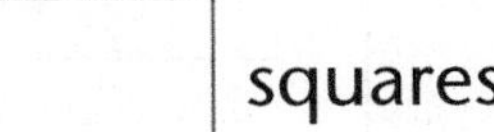

squares

3

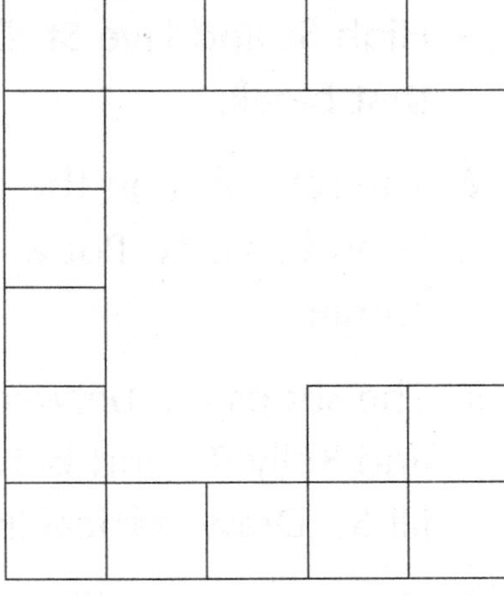

☐ squares

Number and Algebra

SET 1 Basic

1 11 + 6 = ____

2 12 − 5 = ____

3 10 + 4 = ____

4 8 − 3 = ____

5 18 − 7 = ____

6 6 − 3 = ____

7 ____ + 3 = 10

8 19 − 11 = ____

9 1 ten and 9 ones = ____

10 Liam played 16 games of football but lost 7. How many did he win? ____

SET 2 Addition split strategy

Split these numbers into tens and ones to complete these additions.

1 22 + 12 = 30 + 4 = ____

2 23 + 15 = ____ + ____ = ____

3 43 + 14 = ____ + ____ = ____

4 16 + 13 = ____ + ____ = ____

5 24 + 32 = ____ + ____ = ____

6 56 + 12 = ____ + ____ = ____

7 65 + 24 = ____ + ____ = ____

8 42 + 37 = ____ + ____ = ____

9 46 + 32 = ____ + ____ = ____

10 35 + 61 = ____ + ____ = ____

11 72 + 26 = ____ + ____ = ____

12 67 + 30 = ____ + ____ = ____

Space Following directions

1 The park is on the block between Kelly Rd and Hodge St and between High St and Five St. Draw trees on that block.

2 The school is on the corner of Bardot St and Five St. Put a cross on that corner.

3 The shops are between Tom St and Kelly Rd and between Jack St and Jill St. Draw vertical lines on that block.

4 Draw a circle on Tom's house, which is on the corner of Log Rd and Jack St.

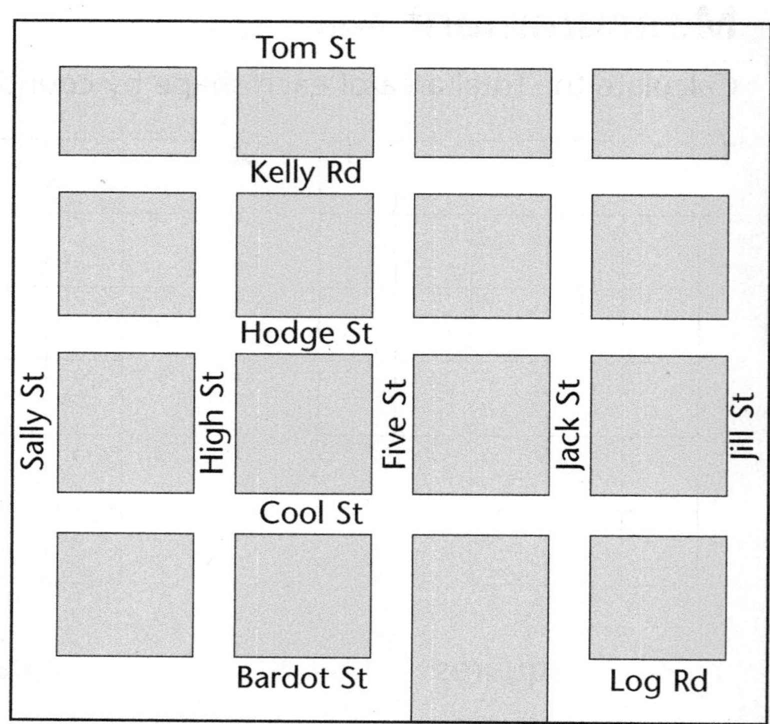

Number and Algebra

SET 3 Halves, quarters and eighths

1 Draw circles to break the group of 8 into halves.

2 Draw circles to break the group of 16 into quarters.

3 Draw circles to break the group of 16 into eighths.

SET 4 Extension

1 How much are 2 kg of potatoes at $2.50 per kilo?

2 3 calculators at $4 each

3 20 + 35

4 ☐ + 12 = 24

5 Half of 80

6 Is 25 an odd number?

7 Kelly saved $5 a month for 10 months. How much did she save?

8 4 lots of 6

9 Is December a summer month?

10 Place the numbers 6, 2, 1 and 7 into the shapes so that each line adds to 13.

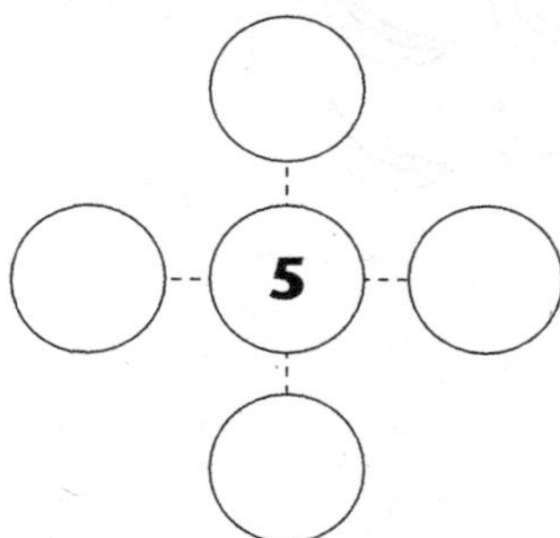

Statistics and Probability Chance

Colour the word that best describes the chance of each event happening.

1 Our school library day is on Saturday.

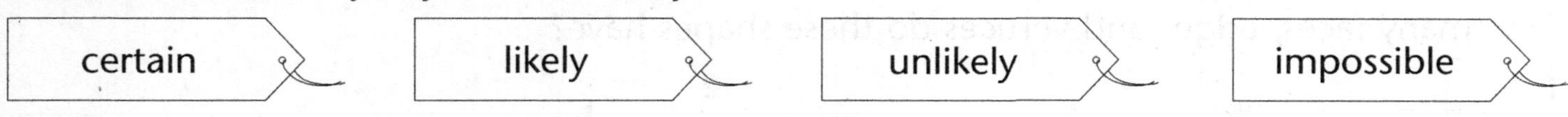

2 Our school assembly day is on Friday.

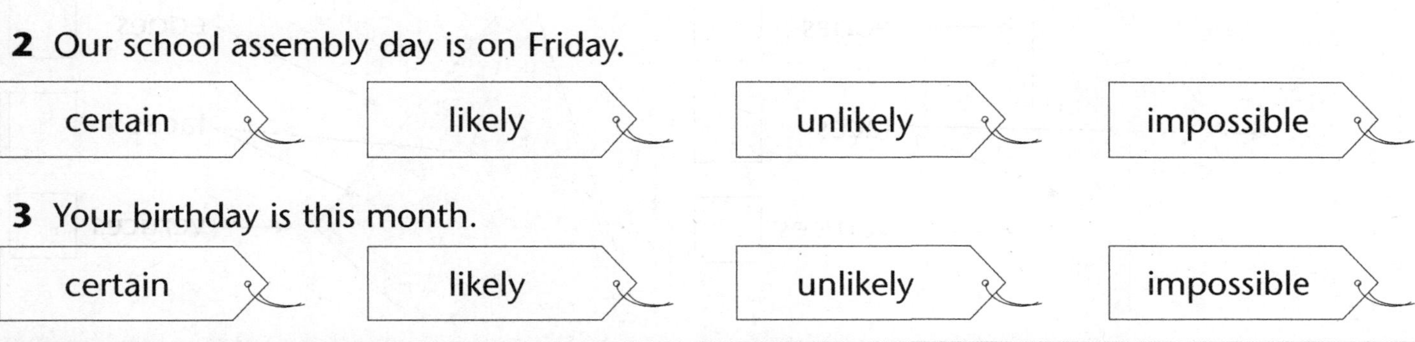

3 Your birthday is this month.

certain | likely | unlikely | impossible

UNIT 29

Number and Algebra

SET 1 Basic

	+ 10	
1	1	
2	2	
3	3	
4	4	
5	5	
6	6	

7 19 − 10 = ☐

8 10 + 10 = ☐

9 20 − 10 = ☐

10 Diab had 6 red lollies and 6 blue lollies. How many does he have altogether? ☐

SET 2 The division symbol – arrays

Show three different ways to divide the groups.

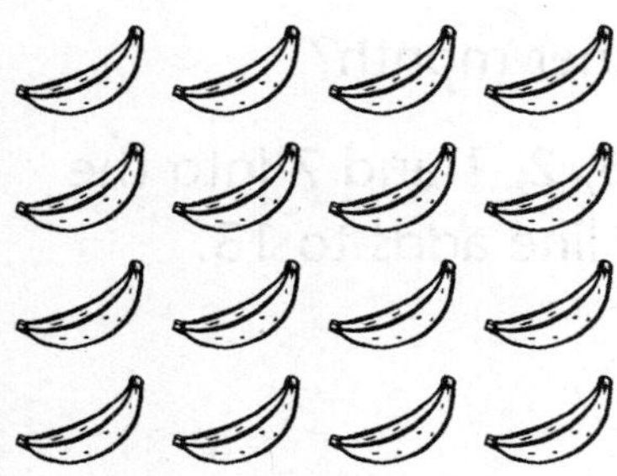

1 16 ÷ 2 = ☐

2 16 ÷ 4 = ☐

3 16 ÷ 8 = ☐

4 20 ÷ 2 = ☐

5 20 ÷ 4 = ☐

6 20 ÷ 5 = ☐

Space Faces, vertices and edges

How many faces, edges and vertices do these shapes have?

1

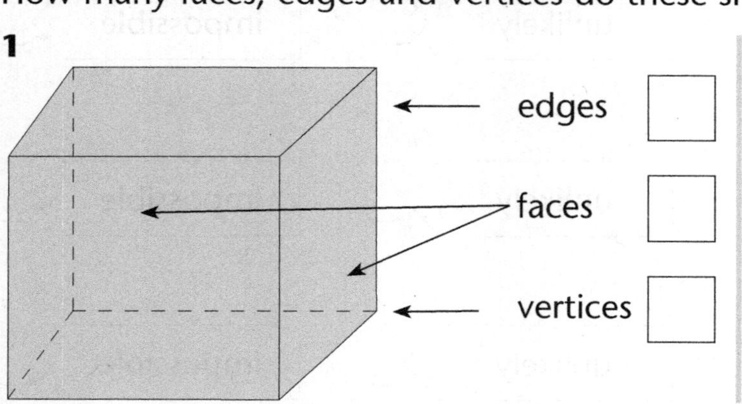

edges ☐

faces ☐

vertices ☐

2

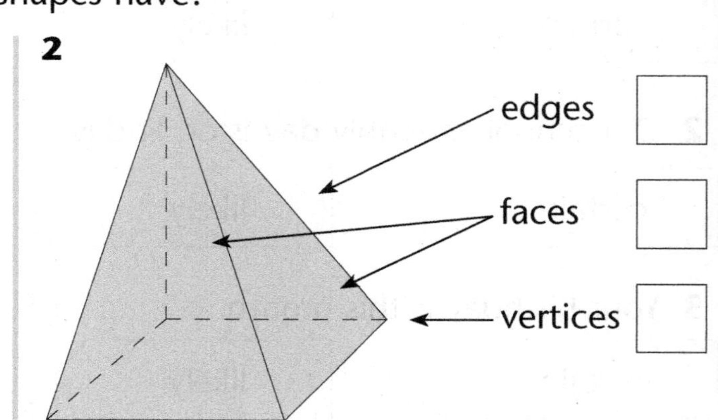

edges ☐

faces ☐

vertices ☐

Number and Algebra

SET 3 Subtraction strategy

Solve the subtractions using any strategy.

1 18 − 8 = ___

2 26 − 8 = ___

3 34 − 6 = ___

4 86 − 42 = ___

5 95 − 37 = ___

6 92 − 27 = ___

7 There were 48 cakes but 23 were eaten. How many cakes were left?

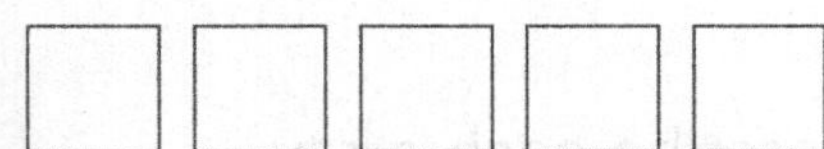

8 There were 56 apples on a tree but 24 were picked. How many apples are left on the tree?

SET 4 Extension

1 10, 15, 20, ____, ____, 35

2 How many centimetres in 3 m?

3 How many sixes = 12?

4 Ian had 36 stickers.
How many groups of 6 can he make?

5 4 + 8 + 3 + 1

6 How many 50c coins make $3?

7 Is a prism a 2D shape?

8 Which is bigger: $\frac{1}{3}$ or $\frac{1}{4}$?

9 Show 9:30 on the clock below.

10 50 km – 19 km

11 Write the number 5 less than 92.

12 Is 63 odd or even?

Measurement Mass

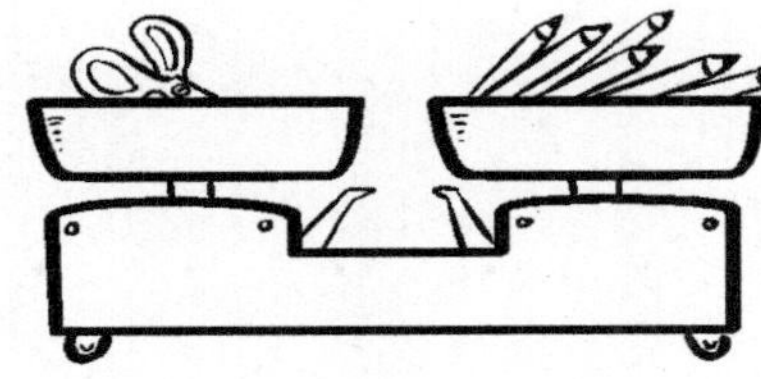

Study the scales above to answer the questions.

1 How many pencils are needed to balance a pair of scissors? ____________

2 How many pencils are needed to balance a calculator? ____________

3 How many pencils are needed to balance 3 pairs of scissors? ____________

UNIT 30

Number and Algebra

SET 1 Basic

1 11 − 2 = ☐

2 6 − 3 = ☐

3 10 + 8 = ☐

4 4 + 4 = ☐

5 8 − 2 = ☐

6 One number after 16 = ☐

7 Double 8 = ☐

8 20c plus 40c = ☐

9 2 tens and 16 ones = ☐

10

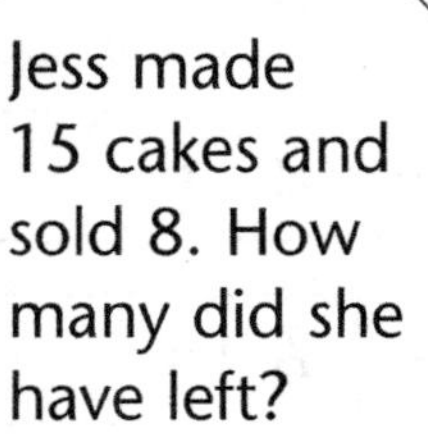

SET 2 Remainders

Write a multiplication sentence and a division sentence to describe each array.

1 There are ☐ groups of 5 with ☐ remainder.

2 There are ☐ groups of 4 with ☐ remainder.

Measurement Centimetres

Use a ruler to draw lines that match the measurements.

1 9 cm

2 12 cm

3 8 cm

4 6 cm

5 14 cm

Number and Algebra

SET 3 Number before and after

Order the numbers from the smallest to the largest.

1 274, 305, 187, 256

2 397, 973, 739, 205

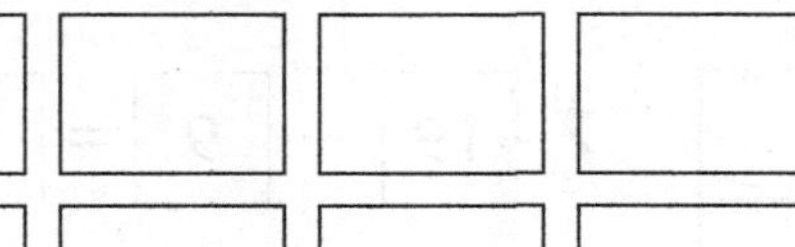

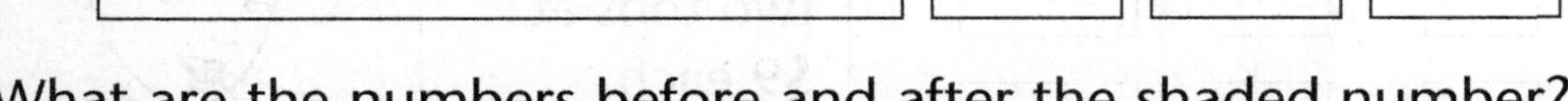

What are the numbers before and after the shaded number?

3 [ ] 59 [ ]

4 [ ] 181 [ ]

5 [ ] 465 [ ]

6 [ ] 743 [ ]

SET 4 Extension

1 100 – 83

2 Half of 60

3 \$2 = [ ] cents

4 Sum of 16 and 3

5 Jackson had 5 boxes each containing 10 apples. How many apples does he have altogether?

6 3 + 3 + 2

7 9 + [ ] = 16

8 25, 50, ____, 100

9 Circle the largest number.
101, 111, 001

10 Enlarge the shape by doubling its dimensions.

Space Shapes within shapes

Write down everything you know about this object. Its net may help you.

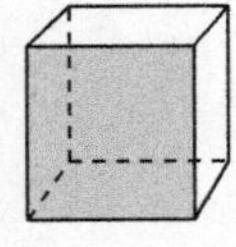

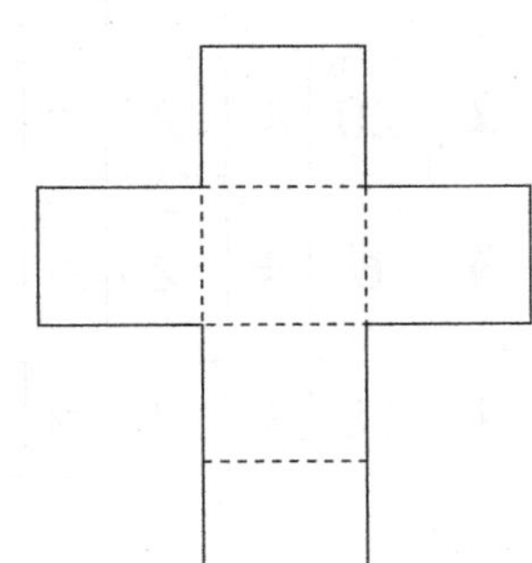

Number and Algebra

SET 1 Basic

		+ 9
1	1	
2	2	
3	3	
4	4	
5	9	
6	11	

7 19 − 9 = ☐

8 10 + 9 = ☐

9 8 + 9 = ☐

10 Jayne bought two tops at $9 each. How much did she spend? ☐

SET 2 Subtraction facts

Complete the spider's webs. The stars may help you.

☆☆☆☆☆☆☆☆☆☆☆☆☆☆☆☆☆☆☆☆

1

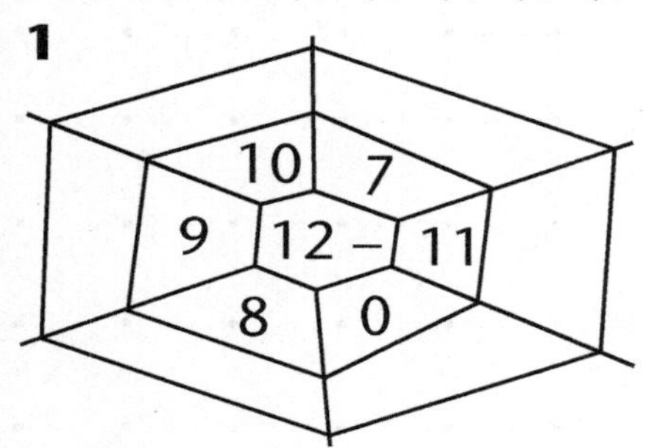

2

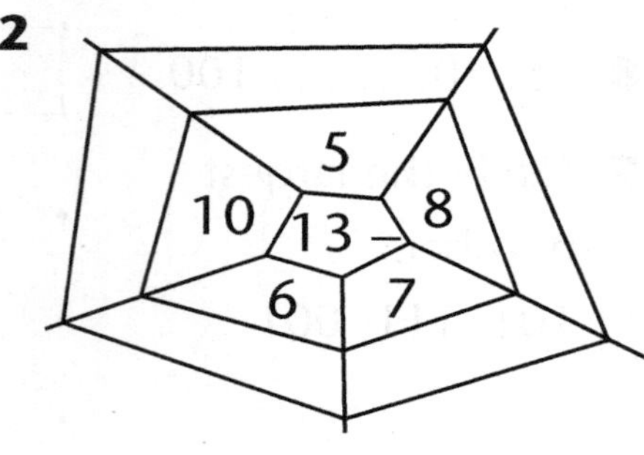

3

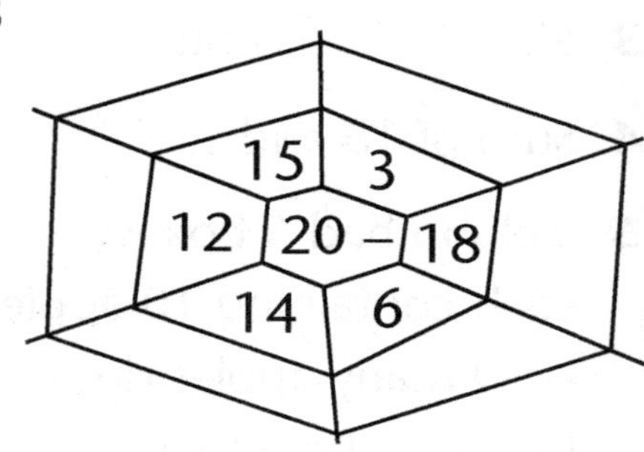

Number and Algebra Division/repeated subtraction

Use the number line to solve the divisions.

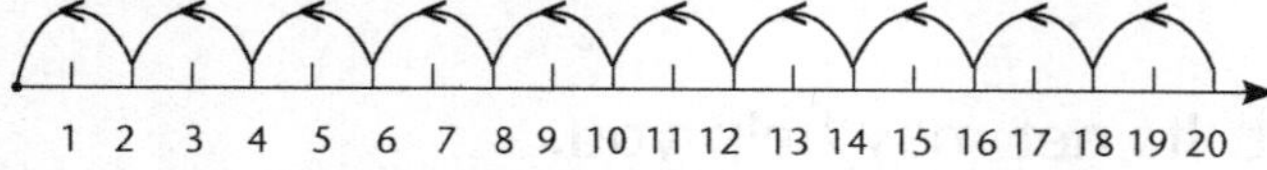

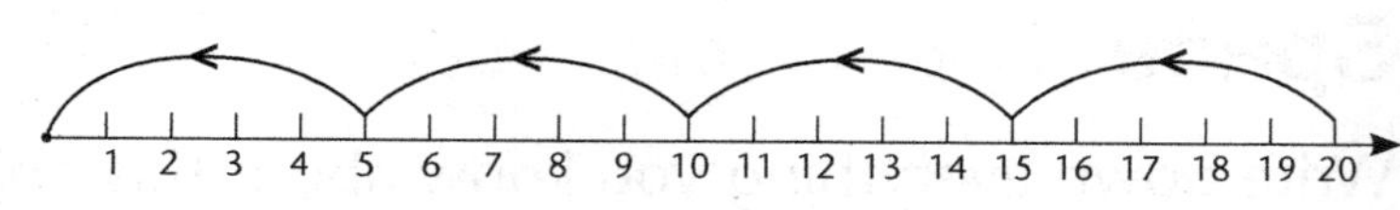

1 14 ÷ 2 = ☐

2 20 ÷ 2 = ☐

3 6 ÷ 2 = ☐

4 18 ÷ 2 = ☐

5 20 ÷ 5 = ☐

6 15 ÷ 5 = ☐

7 10 ÷ 5 = ☐

Number and Algebra

SET 3 Related number sentences

1

7 + 8 =	15
8 + ☐ =	15
15 − 8 =	
15 − ☐ =	8

2

7 + 11 =	
☐ + 7 =	18
18 − 7 =	
18 − ☐ =	7

3 Write two subtraction number sentences that are related to the addition number sentence below.

9 + 6 = 15   15 − ☐ = ☐   ☐ − 9 = ☐

SET 4 Extension

1 Write the largest number you can using 1, 3, 4.

2 How many months in spring?

3 The value of 3 in 392

4 Halves in 2 wholes

5 What 2 coins make 70c?

6 Six lots of six = ☐

7 Write the number for 3 hundreds + 4 tens + 6 ones. ____

8 Add 2 tens to 302.

9 205, 207, __, 211, __

10 Share 35 among 5.

11 Write the smallest number you can using 2, 4, 1.

12 Half of 32

13 Write the number 10 more than 73.

Measurement The calendar

September

S	M	T	W	T	F	S
30						1
2	3	4	5	6	7	8
9	10	11	12	13	14	15
16	17	18	19	20	21	22
23	24	25	26	27	28	29

October

S	M	T	W	T	F	S
	1	2	3	4	5	6
7	8	9	10	11	12	13
14	15	16	17	18	19	20
21	22	23	24	25	26	27
28	29	30	31			

November

S	M	T	W	T	F	S
				1	2	3
4	5	6	7	8	9	10
11	12	13	14	15	16	17
18	19	20	21	22	23	24
25	26	27	28	29	30	

December

S	M	T	W	T	F	S
30	31					1
2	3	4	5	6	7	8
9	10	11	12	13	14	15
16	17	18	19	20	21	22
23	24	25	26	27	28	29

What day of the week is:

1 October 19? ____

2 September 28? ____

3 December 25? ____

4 November 16? ____

5 9 days after November 13? ____

6 14 days after October 7? ____

UNIT 32

Number and Algebra

SET 1 Basic

1 12 − 6 = ☐

2 14 + 4 = ☐

3 19 − 8 = ☐

4 20 − 11 = ☐

5 15 + 5 = ☐

6 10 − 6 = ☐

7 3 × 5 = ☐

8 2 × 9 = ☐

9 Double 8 = ☐

10

Aja had two 20c pieces and 3 $1 coins. How much money did she have?

☐

SET 2 Find the difference

Complete these subtractions to find the secret word.

C	M	E	T	O	P	L
3	4	7	9	2	5	8

1 8 − 5 = ☐

2 9 − 7 = ☐

3 12 − 8 = ☐

4 15 − 10 = ☐

5 14 − 6 = ☐

6 15 − 8 = ☐

7 16 − 7 = ☐

8 17 − 10 = ☐

Secret word

1	2	3	4	5	6	7	8

Space Position

Draw what you would see if you were looking down on this room.

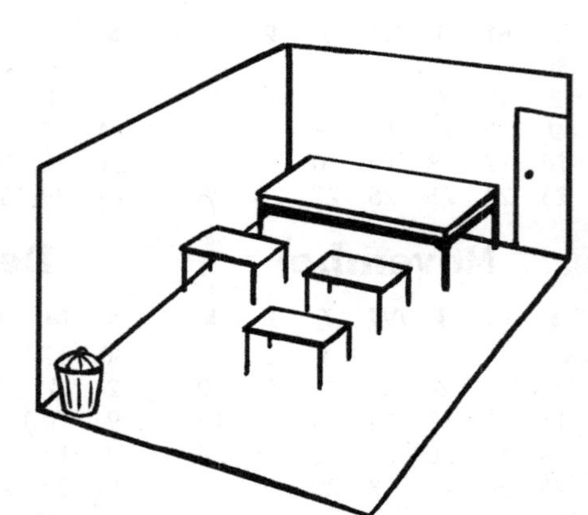

Number and Algebra

SET 3 Quantity value

Record the quantity value of the digit in bold.

1	**3**42	3 represents	300	or	3 hundreds
2	5**8**9	8 represents		or	
3	**7**75	7 represents		or	
4	9**4**1	4 represents		or	

Change the quantity values into three-digit numbers.

5 2 hundreds + 7 tens + 8 becomes ______________

6 7 hundreds + 6 tens + 4 becomes ______________

7 9 hundreds + 0 tens + 2 becomes ______________

SET 4 Extension

1 7 more than 25

2 2 weeks + 3 days = ☐ days

3 200 – 5 =

4 Double 21.

5 50% of 100

6 How many groups of 30 can go into 90?

7 How many minutes in $1\frac{1}{2}$ hours?

8 Round 839 to the nearest 10.

9 Sum of 6 and 27

10 Multiply 5 and 3.

11 Put these numbers in order from smallest to largest.
293, 339, 103, 406, 239, 101

Statistics and Probability Column graphs

Colour the blocks to represent the foods. The first one has been done for you.

Favourite foods of my class

5	■					
4	■					
3	■					
2	■					
1	■					
	strawberry	ice cream	watermelon	burger	cupcake	lolly

Types of food

Maths helpers

Hundreds chart

1	2	3	4	5	6	7	8	9	10
11	12	13	14	15	16	17	18	19	20
21	22	23	24	25	26	27	28	29	30
31	32	33	34	35	36	37	38	39	40
41	42	43	44	45	46	47	48	49	50
51	52	53	54	55	56	57	58	59	60
61	62	63	64	65	66	67	68	69	70
71	72	73	74	75	76	77	78	79	80
81	82	83	84	85	86	87	88	89	90
91	92	93	94	95	96	97	98	99	100

Addition grid

+	0	1	2	3	4	5	6	7	8	9	10	11	12
0	0	1	2	3	4	5	6	7	8	9	10	11	12
1	1	2	3	4	5	6	7	8	9	10	11	12	13
2	2	3	4	5	6	7	8	9	10	11	12	13	14
3	3	4	5	6	7	8	9	10	11	12	13	14	15
4	4	5	6	7	8	9	10	11	12	13	14	15	16
5	5	6	7	8	9	10	11	12	13	14	15	16	17
6	6	7	8	9	10	11	12	13	14	15	16	17	18
7	7	8	9	10	11	12	13	14	15	16	17	18	19
8	8	9	10	11	12	13	14	15	16	17	18	19	20
9	9	10	11	12	13	14	15	16	17	18	19	20	21
10	10	11	12	13	14	15	16	17	18	19	20	21	22
11	11	12	13	14	15	16	17	18	19	20	21	22	23
12	12	13	14	15	16	17	18	19	20	21	22	23	24

Answers

UNIT 1 Number and Algebra

SET 1

1 6
2 5
3 4
4 3
5 7
6 9
7 3
8 2
9 6
10 7

SET 2

1 a / b

7 + 6 = 13   8 + 8 = 16

2 a 6, b 9, c 7, d 10
3 a 7, b 10, c 8, d 11
4 a 10, b 13, c 11, d 14

SET 3

Possible answers

1
2
3
4

SET 4

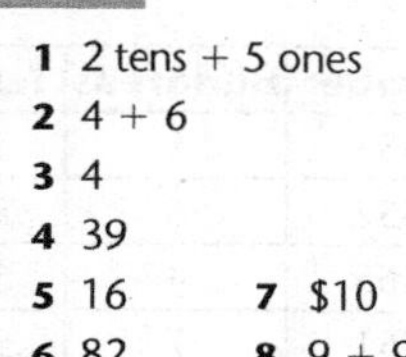

1 2 tens + 5 ones
2 4 + 6
3 4
4 39
5 16
6 82
7 $10
8 9 + 9
9

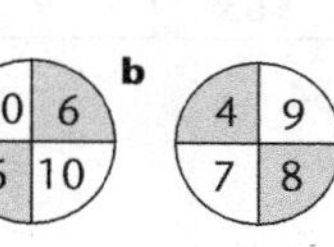

Space

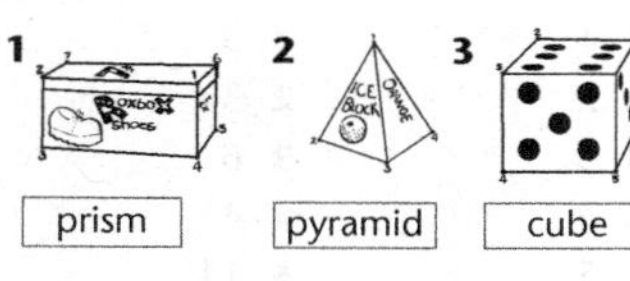

Measurement

1 Pencil = 3 (red)
2 Pen = 4 (yellow)
3 Paint brush = 5 (green)

UNIT 2 Number and Algebra

SET 1

1 3
2 5
3 7
4 8
5 6
6 9
7 8
8 5
9 3
10 5

SET 2

1 14
2 8
3 5
4 5
5 13
6 8

SET 3

1 0, 2, 4, 6, 8, 10, 12
2 0, 4, 8, 12, 16, 20, 24
3 5, 10, 15, 20, 25, 30, 35
4 10, 20, 30, 40, 50, 60, 70
5 10, 12, 14, 16, 18, 20, 22
6 20, 25, 30, 35, 40, 45, 50
7 30, 34, 38, 42, 46, 50, 54
8 50, 55, 60, 65, 70, 75, 80

SET 4

1 16
2 26 January
3 126
4 2
5 5
6 36
7 5 tens 6 ones
8 $10
9 20
10 4th, 5th
11 Hands on, some examples could be:
a 3 + 2
b 1 + 4
c 2 + 3

Space

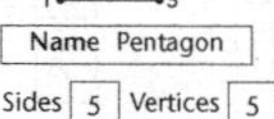

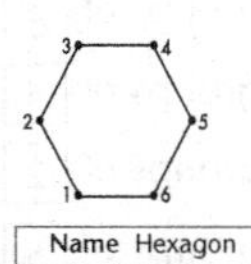

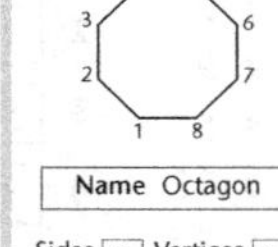

Measurement

1 a red
c green
2 Hands on (by counting squares)

UNIT 3 Number and Algebra

SET 1

1 6
2 5
3 1
4 7
5 4
6 2
7 4
8 4
9 8
10 8

SET 2

1 2, 4, 6, 8, 10
2 5, 10, 15, 20, 25
3 10, 20, 30, 40, 50, 60
4 3, 6, 9, 12, 15

SET 3

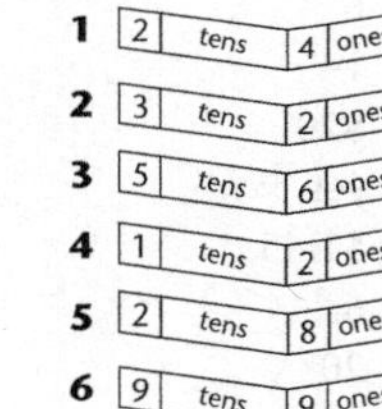
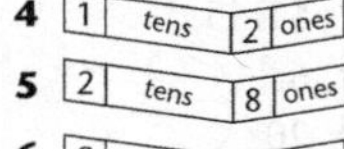

1 2 tens 4 ones
2 3 tens 2 ones
3 5 tens 6 ones
4 1 tens 2 ones
5 2 tens 8 ones
6 9 tens 9 ones
7 63 64 65
8 95 96 97

SET 4

1

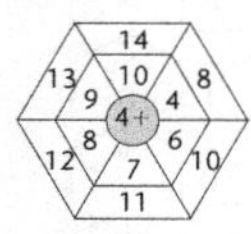

2 winter
3 17
4 15
5 10
6 0
7 31
8 1 tens 8 ones
9 7
10 215, 512, (125)
11 April

Space

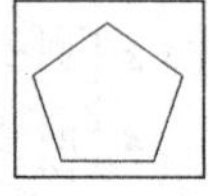
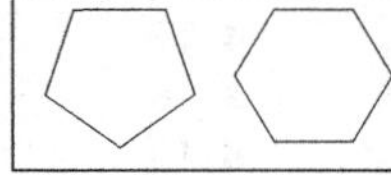

Measurement

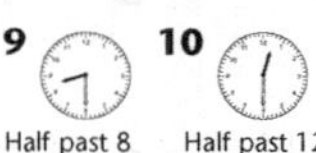

UNIT 4 Number and Algebra

SET 1

1 6
2 8
3 3
4 8
5 5
6 8
7 2
8 1
9 5
10 6

SET 2

1 Red: 6 + 5, 10 + 1
2 Blue: 6 + 6, 5 + 7, 10 + 2
3 Yellow: 11 + 2, 10 + 3, 7 + 6
4 Green: 7 + 7, 12 + 2, 8 + 6, 10 + 4

SET 3

1 3 groups of 3 = 9
2 3 groups of 4 = 12
3 5 groups of 10 = 50
4 6 groups of 2 = 12

SET 4

1 Seven
2 10
3 12
4 Even
5 1 metre
6 14
7 7
8 8
9 30
10 October
11 $3.80

Statistics and Probability

Hands on.

Measurement

Answers

UNIT 5 Number and Algebra

SET 1

1 1
2 2
3 3
4 4
5 5
6 6
7 5
8 7
9 7
10 7

SET 2

1 3
2 3
3 6
4 4
5 11
6 12
7 6
8 9
9 9 years

SET 3

	Number	Hundreds	Tens	Ones
1	533	5	3	3
2	652	6	5	2
3	465	4	6	5
4	751	7	5	1
5	963	9	6	3

6 754
7 457

SET 4

1 31
2 10
3 3 tens 6 ones
4 December
5 13
6 10
7 21
8
9 8 − 2 = 6
10 3 hundreds 5 tens 6 ones
11 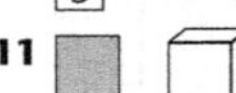
12 12 months

Space

Hands on.

Measurement

Hands on.

UNIT 6 Number and Algebra

SET 1

1 10
2 9
3 9
4 5
5 12
6 5
7 7
8 5
9 2
10 2

SET 2

1 4 groups of 3 = 12
2 4 groups of 4 = 16
3 5 groups of 2 = 10
4 3 groups of 5 = 15

SET 3

1 4 groups of 5
5 + 5 + 5 + 5 = 20
2 2 groups of 7
7 + 7 = 14
3 5 groups of 3
3 + 3 + 3 + 3 + 3 = 15
4 3 groups of 3
3 + 3 + 3 = 9

SET 4

1 Numerous responses
2 26, 28
3 6
4 Autumn
5 7 + 3 = 10
6 9
7 3
8 15c
9 Equal in weight
10 5c
11 20
12 25 April
13 6

Statistics and Probability

1 Yellow
2 No
3 Red
4 No

Statistics and Probability

1

Cat	IIII	Bird	IIII
Dog	𝍸 I	Lizard	I
Fish	III		

2 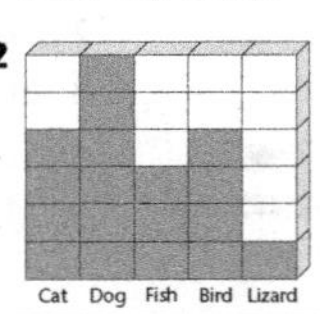

UNIT 7 Number and Algebra

SET 1

1 4
2 5
3 6
4 7
5 8
6 9
7 5
8 10
9 8
10 4

SET 2

1 11
2 9
3 11
4 12
5 16
6 15
7 11
8 14
9 14
10 12

SET 3

1 6 hundreds 5 tens 8 ones
2 7 hundreds 3 tens 4 ones
3 5 hundreds 4 tens 1 ones
4 8 hundreds 6 tens 6 ones
5 9 hundreds 7 tens 9 ones
6 Hund Tens Ones: 5 6 4
7 Hund Tens Ones: 8 9 7

SET 4

1 10, 13, 23, 99
2 14
3 6
4 14
5 $20
6 yes
7 $1.65
8 6
9 20
10 8
11 Hands on.

Space

1 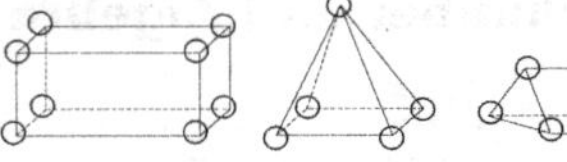
2 Hands on.

Measurement

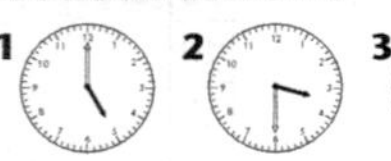

1 5 o'clock
2 Half past 3
3 Half past 9
4 Half past 7
5 Half past 10
6 7 o'clock
7 Half past 11
8 Half past 6

UNIT 8 Number and Algebra

SET 1

1 5
2 4
3 1
4 4
5 8
6 5
7 6
8 8
9 8
10 5

SET 2

1 14
2 16
3 19
4 22
5 10
6 12
7 18
8 25

SET 3

1 2
2 4
3 6
4 10
5 12
6 16
7 2
8 3
9 6
10 5
11 7
12 10

SET 4

1 Three hundred and ten
2 9
3 4
4 15
5 8
6 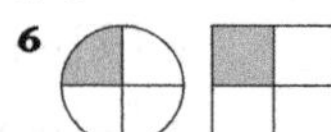
7 31 days
8 2 halves
9 299
10 100
11 April
12

+	3	6	9	12	15	18	21
3	6	9	12	15	18	21	24

Space

Σ	O	Z	⋊	Ш	≻
M	O	N	K	E	Y

Measurement

1 8 shoes
2 6 shoe boxes

Answers

UNIT 9 Number and Algebra

SET 1

1 1
2 2
3 3
4 4
5 5
6 6
7 11
8 9
9 7
10 5

SET 2

1 [3] groups of [3]
2 [4] groups of [4]
3 [5] groups of [5]
4 [3] groups of [5]
5 [7] groups of [2]

SET 3

1 [4] + [11] = [15]
2 [12] + [6] = [18]
3 [19] − [4] = [15]
4 [16] − [3] = [13]

SET 4

1 9
2 40
3 6
4 6
5 24, 26, 28
6 [2] tens [7] ones
7 100
8 12
9 Hands on.
10 8
11 December
12 17
13 69

Space

1 triangle
2 square
3 rectangle
4 octagon
5 hexagon
6 pentagon

Measurement

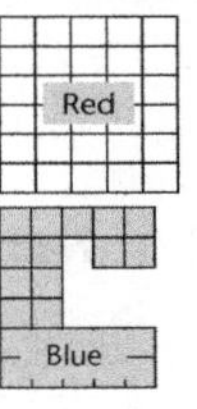

UNIT 10 Number and Algebra

SET 1

1 5
2 12
3 7
4 5
5 6
6 8
7 8
8 4
9 5
10 6 pets

SET 2

1 Card b wins.
2 13
3 11
4 18
5 17
6 15
7 16
8 20
9 14
10 18

SET 3

1 28 + 2 + 7 = 37
2 49 + 1 + 7 = 57
3 37 + 3 + 3 = 43
4 16 + 4 + 4 = 24
5 35 + 5 + 3 = 43

SET 4

1 36
2 21
3 13 + 2
4 3 months
5 15
6 24
7 80c
8 23
9 2, 4, 6, 8, 10, 12, 14
10 24
11 26 December
12 13
13 21
14 14

Space

1 Car
2 Piggy bank
3 Clock
4 Soldier
5 Doll

Measurement

1 1 minute
2 1 hour
3 5 minutes

UNIT 11 Number and Algebra

SET 1

1 5
2 6
3 7
4 8
5 9
6 10
7 15
8 10
9 10
10 14

SET 2

1 9
2 3
3 11
4 7
5 6
6 8
7 19
8 10
9 9
10 7

SET 3

Hands on.

SET 4

1 52, 62, 72, 82, 92, 102
2 4
3 15
4 $\frac{2}{4}$ or $\frac{1}{2}$
5 12
6 6
7 50c
8 30
9 34, 44, 54, 64, 74, 84
10 90
11 100 cm
12 2 dozen
13 10, 13, 22, 23, 43, 83

Space

1 2 hexagons and 6 rectangles
2 1 square and 4 triangles

Measurement

1 Tom
2 Sally

UNIT 12 Number and Algebra

SET 1

1 16
2 12
3 6
4 6
5 6
6 10
7 5
8 15
9 12
10 15 cows

SET 2

1 [6] rows of [3] = 18
[3] columns of [6] = 18
2 [5] rows of [4] = 20
[4] columns of [5] = 20
3 24
4 24
5 35
6 30

SET 3

1 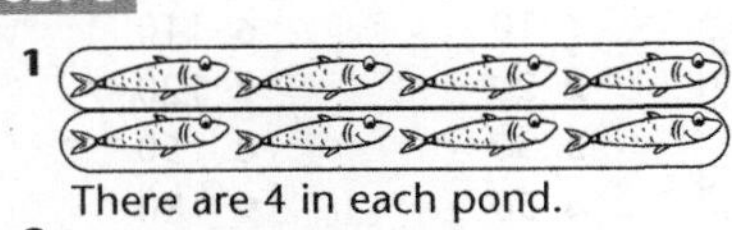
There are 4 in each pond.

2 
There are 5 in each pond.

3 
There are 6 in each group.

SET 4

1 Winter
2 6
3 57
4 110 cents
5 30
6 6
7 5
8 76
9 30
10 40, 44, 48, 52, 56
11 31 days
12 55
13 8 legs
14 88

Statistics and Probability

1 Blond
2 Black
3 3
4 1

Measurement

1 Mug
2 Paint can
3 Cordial bottle
4 Saucepan

Answers

UNIT 13 Number and Algebra

SET 1

1 6
2 8
3 10
4 14
5 16
6 18
7 13
8 1
9 4
10 15

SET 2

1 15 + 15 = 30 (number line: 25, 30)
2 32 + 19 = 51 (number line: 42, 51)
3 28 + 24 = 52 (number line: 48, 52)

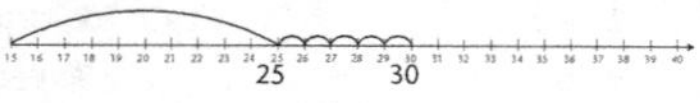

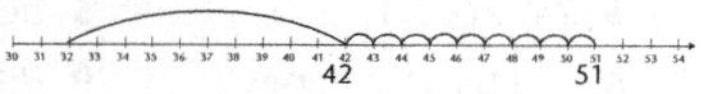

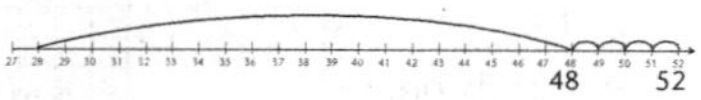

SET 3

1 | 86 | 88 | 90 | 92 | 94 | 96 |
2 | 10 | 14 | 18 | 22 | 26 | 30 |
3 | 85 | 90 | 95 | 100 | 105 | 110 |
4 | 12 | 14 | 16 | 18 | 20 | 22 |
5 | 205 | 210 | 215 | 220 | 225 | 230 |
6 | 32 | 34 | 36 | 38 | 40 | 42 | 44 | 46 | 48 |
7 | 25 | 30 | 35 | 40 | 45 | 50 | 55 | 60 | 65 |
8 | 85 | 80 | 75 | 70 | 65 | 60 | 55 | 50 | 45 |
9 | 86 | 84 | 82 | 80 | 78 | 76 | 74 | 72 | 70 |

SET 4

1 31
2 9
3 83
4 3 sides
5 21 sides
6 24 hours
7 September
8 48
9 ■■■□ 
10 April
11 $1.50
12 46
13 74
14 3rd

Number and Algebra

1 | 47 | 48 | 49 | 50 | 51 |
2 | 12 | 15 | 18 | 21 | 24 |
3 | 85 | 80 | 75 | 70 | 65 |
4 | 97 | 95 | 93 | 91 | 89 |

Measurement

1 7
2 13
3 6
4 Yes

UNIT 14 Number and Algebra

SET 1

1 8
2 4
3 11
4 12
5 6
6 4
7 8
8 6
9 8
10 12

SET 2

1 9 + 5 = 14 → 14 − 5 = 9
2 8 + 7 = 15 → 15 − 7 = 8
3 14 + 8 = 22 → 22 − 8 = 14
4 19 + 12 = 31 → 31 − 12 = 19
5 18 + 16 = 34 → 34 − 16 = 18

SET 3

1 34 + 20 + 5 = 59
2 33 + 10 + 4 = 47
3 36 + 20 + 3 = 59
4 44 + 20 + 5 = 69
5 55 + 30 + 2 = 87

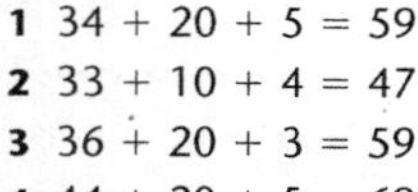

6

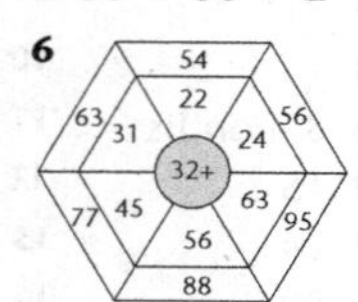

SET 4

1

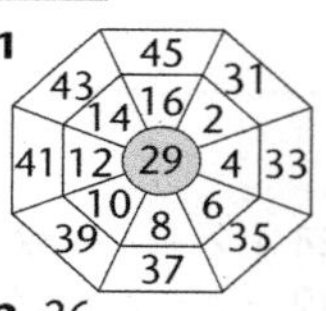

2 26
3 Odd
4 302
5 67
6 24
7 20
8 60
9 36
10 $3.50
11 9 tens 8 ones
12 ♡♡♡♥♡♡♡♡♡

Space

1

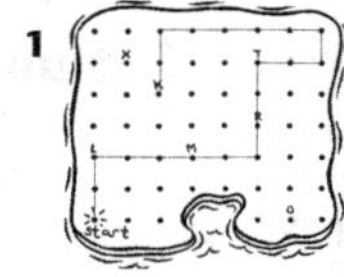

2 K

Statistics and Probability

1 blue
2 red
3 1
4 15

UNIT 15 Number and Algebra

SET 1

1 7
2 9
3 10
4 12
5 15
6 20
7 9
8 6
9 7
10 6

SET 2

1 6
2 10
3 12
4 14
5 16
6 3
7 8
8 (apples drawn in two groups)

SET 3

1 9 − 4 = 5
2 4 + 5 = 9
3 14 − 6 = 8
4 6 + 8 = 14
5 11 − 3 = 8
6 3 + 8 = 11
7 10 − 5 = 5
8 5 + 5 = 10

SET 4

1 12
2 78
3 12 midnight
4 23
5 Summer
6 22
7 5 lollies each
8 7 tens 8 ones
9 38
10 12
11 18
12 1/2
13 48
14 Even

Space

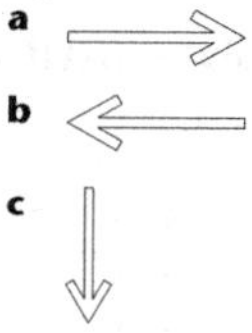

a
b
c

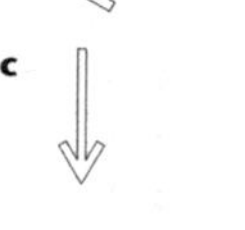

Measurement

1 2 3

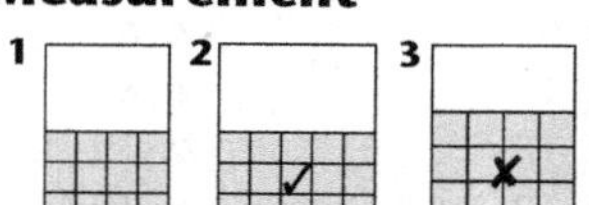

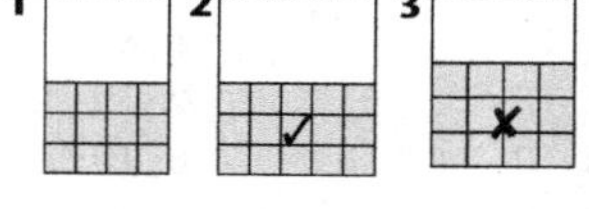

UNIT 16 Number and Algebra

SET 1

1 8
2 2
3 10
4 13
5 15
6 10
7 13
8 6
9 5
10 10

SET 2

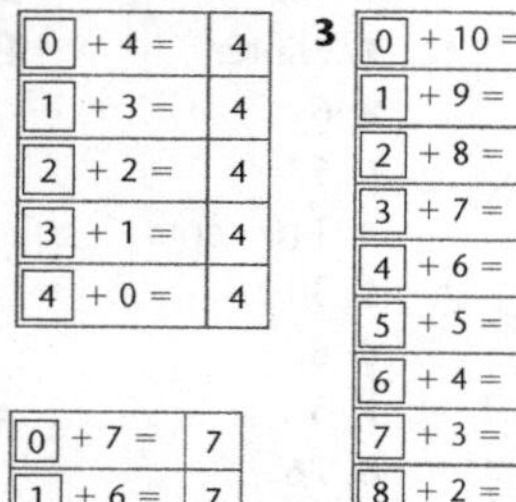

1

0 + 4 =	4
1 + 3 =	4
2 + 2 =	4
3 + 1 =	4
4 + 0 =	4

2

0 + 7 =	7
1 + 6 =	7
2 + 5 =	7
3 + 4 =	7
4 + 3 =	7
5 + 2 =	7
6 + 1 =	7
7 + 0 =	7

3

0 + 10 =	10
1 + 9 =	10
2 + 8 =	10
3 + 7 =	10
4 + 6 =	10
5 + 5 =	10
6 + 4 =	10
7 + 3 =	10
8 + 2 =	10
9 + 1 =	10
10 + 0 =	10

SET 3

1 10
2 20
3 30
4 50
5 60
6 110
7 120
8 150
9 180
10 190

SET 4

1

+	1	2	3	4	10	11
9	10	11	12	13	19	20

2 75
3 365/366 in a leap year
4 12 legs
5 26
6 6 months
7 140
8 10
9 50
10 18 sides
11 12
12 9
13 $335

Statistics and Probability

1 1
2 4
3 2 and 5
4 3

Measurement

	Object	Less than 1 metre	About 1 metre	More than 1 metre
1	The length of your desk	Hands on.		
2	The height of a door			
3	The width of your bedroom			
4	The height of your teacher			
5	The height of your desk	Hands on.		
6	Your height	Hands on.		

Answers

UNIT 17 Number and Algebra

SET 1

1 0
2 2
3 3
4 5
5 7
6 12
7 10
8 13
9 15
10 15

SET 2

1 12
2 16
3 10
4 15
5 24
6 25
7 18
8 28

SET 3

1 3
2 4
3 7
4 Space Land
5 Banana Grove

SET 4

1 14
2 2 days
3 $1.35
4 14
5 22
6 300, 400, 500, 600, 700
7 $1.80
8 $2.50
9 23
10 50
11 8, 6, 4, 2
12 13
13 ♡♥♡♥♡♡♡ Red Blue

Space

1 Cylinder
2 Pyramid
3 Cube
4 Cube and prism

Measurement

1 
Quarter past 7

2 
Quarter to 2

3 
Quarter past 1

4 
Quarter to 4

5 
Quarter to 3

UNIT 18 Number and Algebra

SET 1

1 6
2 6
3 7
4 5
5 5
6 10
7 12
8 no
9 8
10 13

SET 2

1 [2] rows of [5] = [10]
2 [3] rows of [4] = [12]
3 [4] rows of [4] = [16]
4 [3] rows of [6] = [18]

SET 3

1 6
2 3
3 2

SET 4

1 Even
2 7
3 2
4 16
5 11
6 48
7 4:30
8 $1.50
9 9 tens 5 ones
10 330
11 Monday
12 2 dozen
13 40

Space

a 

b c 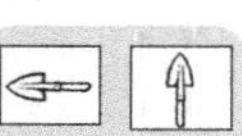

Measurement

1 2 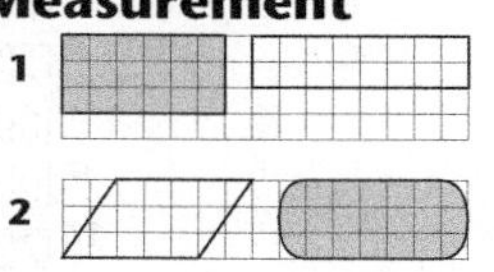

UNIT 19 Number and Algebra

SET 1

1 7
2 8
3 9
4 10
5 11
6 16
7 4
8 12
9 6
10 6

SET 2

1 6
2 10
3 12
4 15
5 17
6 60
7 100
8 120
9 150
10 170
11 $80

SET 3

1 2
2 4
3 3
4 4
5 3
6 7

SET 4

1 17
2 972
3 76
4 $4.50
5 134
6 7 tens
7 3
8 Rule: Add 10
9 100
10 97
11 77
12 6
13

–	10	13	16	19	20	50
3	7	10	13	16	17	47

Space

1 2 3 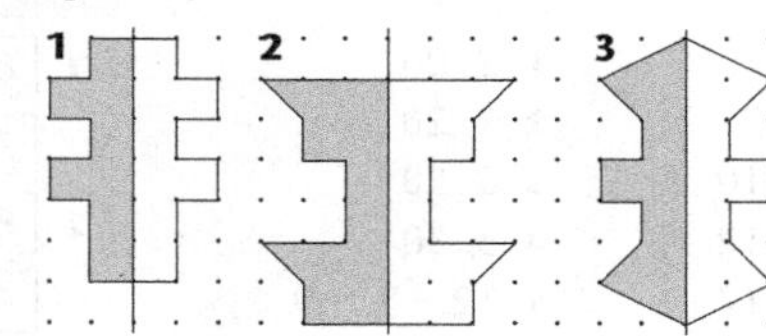

Measurement

Hands on.

UNIT 20 Number and Algebra

SET 1

1 0
2 10
3 3
4 17
5 10
6 15
7 10
8 12
9 9
10 $11

SET 2

1 [2] rows of [2] = [4]
[2] × [2] = [4]
2 [4] rows of [2] = [8]
[4] × [2] = [8]
3 [5] rows of [2] = [10]
[5] × [2] = [10]
4 [6] rows of [2] = [12]
[6] × [2] = [12]
5 [8] rows of [2] = [16]
[8] × [2] = [16]

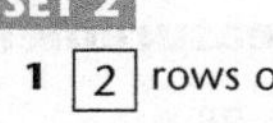

SET 3

1 20
2 30
3 30
4 20
5 40
6 50
7 90
8 40
9 50
10 50
11 60
12 70
13 40
14 50
15 50
16 60
17 80
18 70

SET 4

1 22
2 $13
3 21
4 8
5 120, add 10
6 56
7 5
8 24
9 40
10 678
11 876
12 a 32 b 41

Statistics and Probability

Cleaning materials 𝍸	Tools 𝍸	Food 𝍸 ||

Measurement

0 1 metre 2 metres

Answers

UNIT 21 Number and Algebra

SET 1

1 1
2 2
3 6
4 11
5 12
6 16
7 10
8 10
9 14
10 $11

SET 2

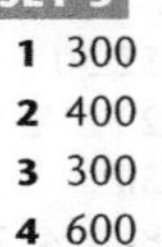
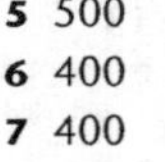

1 8 + 6 | 4 + 10
2 9 + 8 | 6 + 11
3 9 + 6 | 3 + 12
4 20 − 4 | 18 − 2
5 11 − 7 | 15 − 11
6 18 − 5 | 15 − 2

SET 3

1 300
2 400
3 300
4 600
5 500
6 400
7 400
8 400
9 500
10 300
11 700
12 700

SET 4

1
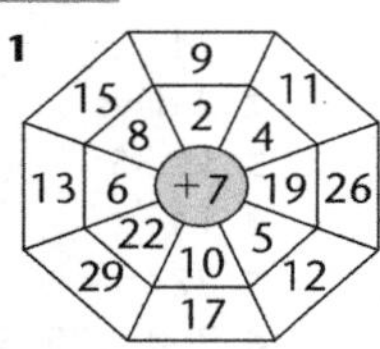

2 $2.50
3 90
4 10
5 Even
6 13, 15, 17, 19, 21, 23
7 0
8 4
9 Hands on.
10 Hands on.

Space

1–6
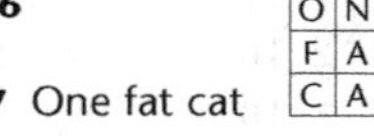

7 One fat cat

Measurement

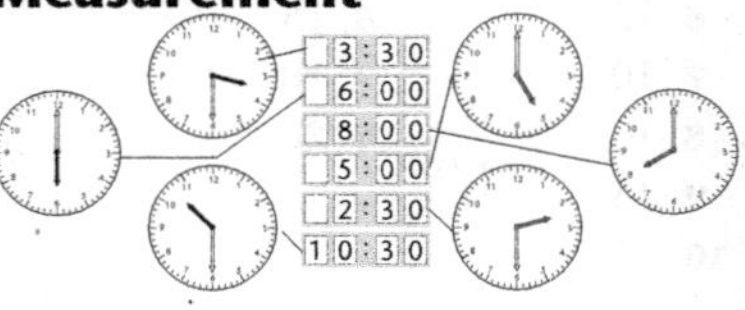

UNIT 22 Number and Algebra

SET 1

1 5
2 5
3 4
4 11
5 19
6 2
7 10
8 20
9 yes
10 17

SET 2

1 12, 120
2 13, 130
3 14, 140
4 15, 150
5 16, 160
6 17, 170

SET 3

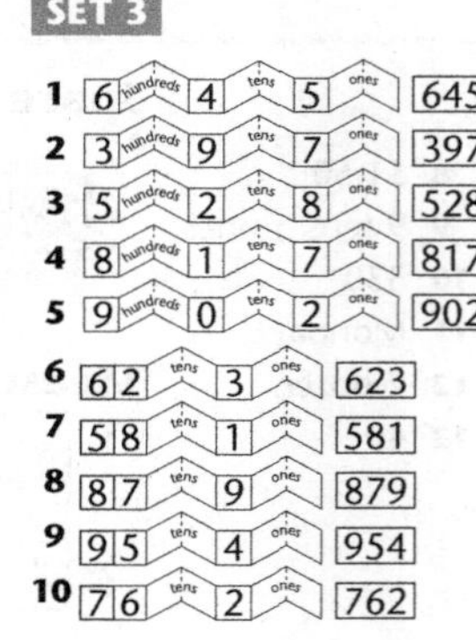

SET 4

1 18
2 19
3 20
4 $9.50
5 50
6 16 legs
7 70 or 7 tens
8 2
9 6
10 4
11
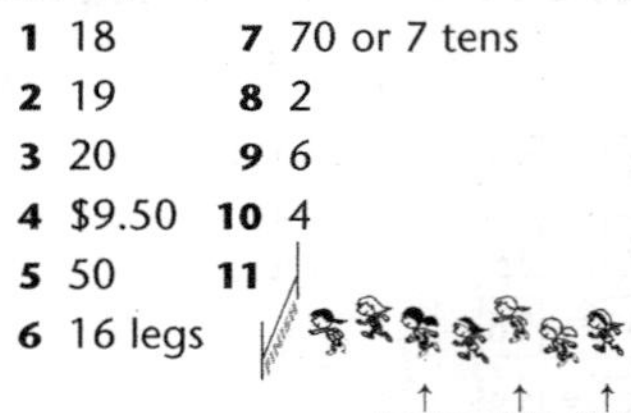

Space

1
2
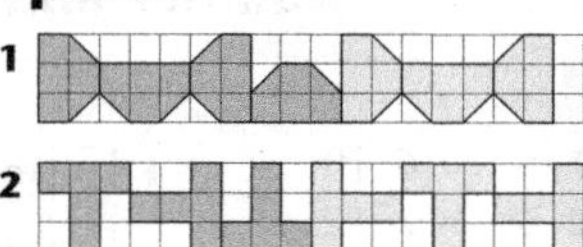

Statistics and Probability

red	☺	☺	☺	☺				
brown	☺	☺	☺	☺	☺	☺	☺	☺
fair	☺	☺	☺	☺	☺			
black	☺	☺	☺	☺	☺	☺		
blond	☺	☺	☺					

UNIT 23 Number and Algebra

SET 1

1 8
2 9
3 10
4 12
5 17
6 20
7 10
8 10
9 17
10 $5

SET 2

1 2, 20
2 2, 20
3 5, 50
4 3, 30
5 12 − 3 = 9
6 120 − 30 = 90

SET 3

1 8 + 7 = 15
7 + 8 = 15
2 8 + 6 = 14
6 + 8 = 14
3 3 × 5 = 15
5 × 3 = 15

SET 4

1 $\frac{1}{2}$
2 52 weeks
3 21
4 48
5 5
6 24
7 24
8 15
9 3 o'clock
10 $1.25
11 $5.25
12 13

Space

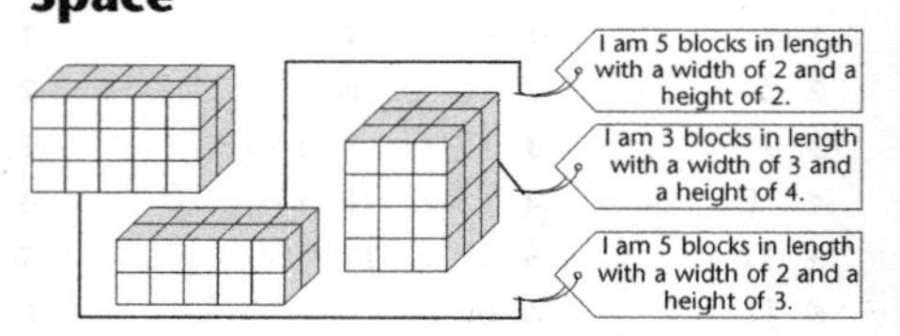

Measurement

1 Put a cross on the arrow.
2 Circle the ruler.
3 Tick the brush.

UNIT 24 Number and Algebra

SET 1

1 10
2 4
3 8
4 10
5 15
6 18
7 5
8 19
9 14
10 17

SET 2

1 8
2 4
3 2

SET 3

1 12 + 7 = 19
2 7 + 8 + 3 = 18
3 20 − 12 = 8
4 24 − 10 = 14
5 16 − 4 = 12

SET 4

1 16
2 60
3 $7
4 $2.75
5 $4
6 75c
7 3
8 1 kg
9 60 minutes
10 90
11 20 ÷ 4 = 5
12 90 or 9 tens
13 7 + 6 = 13
14 12 legs

Measurement

1 28
2 Thursday
3 Sunday, (February 15)
4 February 20
5 Monday, February 23

Measurement

1 8
2 12
3 16
4 10

Answers

UNIT 25 Number and Algebra

SET 1

1 0
2 2
3 3
4 5
5 10
6 15
7 15
8 12
9 7
10 12

SET 2

1 + 4 + 10 = 14
2 + 7 + 10 = 17
3 + 8 + 10 = 18
4 + 1 + 10 = 11

SET 3

1 (5)–(4), (9)
2 (8)–(9), (17)
3 (11)–(5), (16)

4

4 + 3	7	5 + 2	7	6 + 1	7

5

8 + 5	13	10 + 3	13	11 + 2	13

SET 4

1 Twenty-nine
2 30
3 17
4 18
5 Square, rectangle
6 21 days
7 12
8 2 kg feathers
9 $5
10 80 or 8 tens
11

Space

1
2
3

Measurement

Summer	Spring	Winter	Autumn
December	September	June	March
January	October	July	April
February	November	August	May

UNIT 26 Number and Algebra

SET 1

1 16
2 12
3 3
4 11
5 5
6 2
7 $10
8 18
9 7
10 $15

SET 2

1 13
2 16
3 21
4 15
5 15
6 24
7 24
8 27
9 13
10 23

SET 3

1 Colour 1 pear
2 Colour 2 oranges
3 Colour 1 strawberry
4 Colour 2 stars

SET 4

1 10
2 8
3 24
4 20
5 $25
6 366 days
7 13, 15, 17, 19, 21
8 42
9 100
10 Odd
11 23
12 $3.85

Measurement

1 14 cm
2 11 cm
3 13 cm
4 6 cm
5 15 cm

Statistics and Probability

1 12
2 7
3 8
4 Hands on.

UNIT 27 Number and Algebra

SET 1

1 9
2 10
3 13
4 15
5 18
6 19
7 12
8 20
9 14
10 7

SET 2

1 10
2 50
3 15
4 20
5 25
6 40
7 35
8 30

SET 3

1 5 + 5 + 5 = 15
2 4 + 4 + 4 + 4 = 16

SET 4

1 12
2 25%
3 50%
4 83
5 3 x 7
6 Jenna is 10.
7 8 + 5 = 13
8 $2
9 5 times
10 1000 grams
11 300
12 45

Space

1 Quarter turn
2 Full turn
3 Half turn

Measurement

1 25 squares
2 18 squares
3 16 squares

UNIT 28 Number and Algebra

SET 1

1 17
2 7
3 14
4 5
5 11
6 3
7 7
8 8
9 19
10 9 wins

SET 2

1 30 + 4 = 34
2 30 + 8 = 38
3 50 + 7 = 57
4 20 + 9 = 29
5 50 + 6 = 56
6 60 + 8 = 68
7 80 + 9 = 89
8 70 + 9 = 79
9 70 + 8 = 78
10 90 + 6 = 96
11 90 + 8 = 98
12 90 + 7 = 97

SET 3

1 Circle into 2 groups of 4
2 Circle into 4 groups of 4
3 Circle into 8 groups of 2

SET 4

1 $5
2 $12
3 55
4 12 + 12 = 24
5 40
6 Yes
7 $50
8 24
9 Yes
10 Possible answers

2 / 7 5 1 / 6	1 / 2 5 6 / 7
7 / 6 5 2 / 1	6 / 1 5 7 / 2

Space

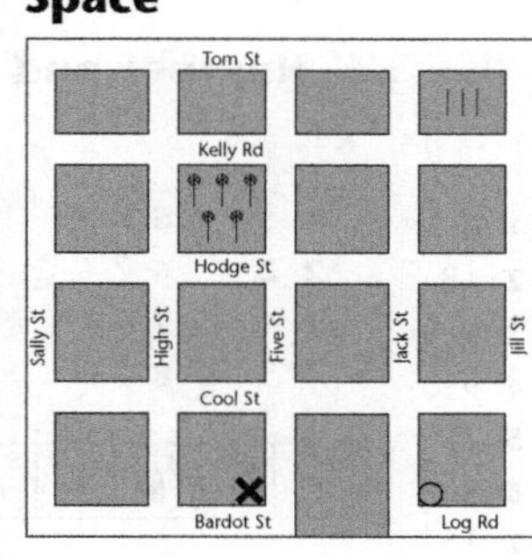

Statistics and Probability

Hands on.

Answers

UNIT 29 Number and Algebra

SET 1

1 11
2 12
3 13
4 14
5 15
6 16
7 9
8 20
9 10
10 12

SET 2

1 8
2 4
3 2
4 10
5 5
6 4

SET 3

1 10
2 18
3 28
4 44
5 58
6 65
7 25
8 32

SET 4

1 10, 15, 20, 25, 30, 35
2 300 cm
3 2
4 6
5 16
6 6
7 No
8 $\frac{1}{3}$
9 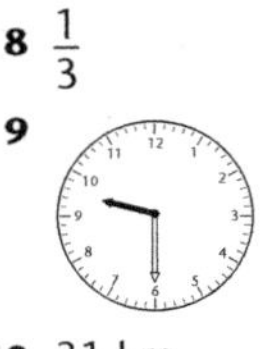
10 31 km
11 87
12 Odd

Space

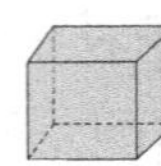
12 edges
6 faces
8 vertices

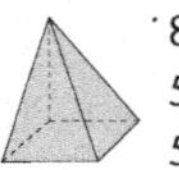
8 edges
5 faces
5 vertices

Measurement

1 6
2 12
3 18

UNIT 30 Number and Algebra

SET 1

1 9
2 3
3 18
4 8
5 6
6 17
7 16
8 60c
9 36
10 7

SET 2

1 There are 3 groups of 5 with 4 remainder.
2 There are 4 groups of 4 with 2 remainder.

SET 3

1 187, 256, 274, 305
2 205, 397, 739, 973
3 58 59 60
4 180 181 182
5 464 465 466
6 742 743 744

SET 4

1 17
2 30
3 200 cents
4 19
5 50
6 8
7 9 + 7 = 16
8 25, 50, 75, 100
9 101, (111), 001
10 Hands on.

Measurement

Hands on.

Space

Hands on. Features include:
6 square faces
12 edges
8 vertices
cube

UNIT 31 Number and Algebra

SET 1

1 10
2 11
3 12
4 13
5 18
6 20
7 10
8 19
9 17
10 $18

SET 2

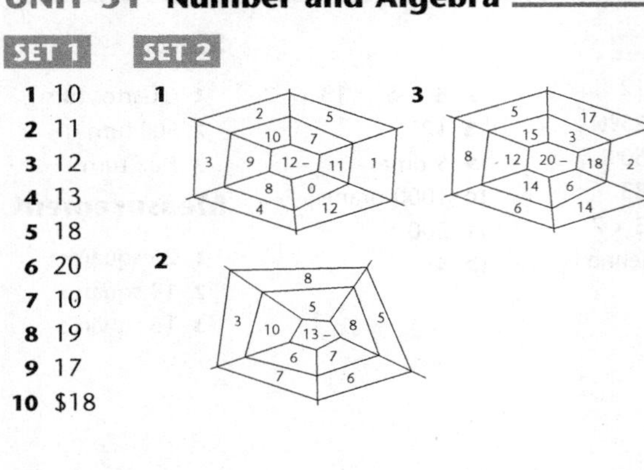

SET 3

1
7 + 8 = 15
8 + 7 = 15
15 − 8 = 7
15 − 7 = 8

2
7 + 11 = 18
11 + 7 = 18
18 − 7 = 11
18 − 11 = 7

3
15 − 6 = 9
15 − 9 = 6

SET 4

1 431
2 3
3 300 or 3 hundreds
4 4
5 50c and 20c
6 36
7 346
8 322
9 205, 207, 209, 211, 213
10 7 each
11 124
12 16
13 83

Number and Algebra

1 7
2 10
3 3
4 9
5 4
6 3
7 2

Measurement

1 Friday
2 Friday
3 Tuesday
4 Friday
5 Thursday
6 Sunday

UNIT 32 Number and Algebra

SET 1

1 6
2 18
3 9
4 9
5 20
6 4
7 15
8 18
9 16
10 $3.40

SET 2

1 3
2 2
3 4
4 5
5 8
6 7
7 9
8 7

1	2	3	4	5	6	7	8
C	O	M	P	L	E	T	E

SET 3

1 300 or 3 hundreds
2 80 or 8 tens
3 700 or 7 hundreds
4 40 or 4 tens
5 278
6 764
7 902

SET 4

1 32
2 17 days
3 195
4 42
5 50
6 3
7 90
8 840
9 33
10 15
11 101, 103, 239, 293, 339, 406

Space

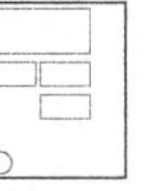

Statistics and Probability

Favourite foods of my class

5
4
3
2
1

Types of food